PLAY BALL
Like the HALL OF FAMERS

PLAY BALL
Like the HALL OF FAMERS
THE INSIDE SCOOP FROM 19 BASEBALL GREATS

To Ryan,

Play Ball! Have Fun!!

Steven Krasner

WRITTEN BY STEVEN KRASNER

ILLUSTRATED BY KEITH NEELY

PEACHTREE
ATLANTA

Ω

Published by
PEACHTREE PUBLISHERS
1700 Chattahoochee Avenue
Atlanta, Georgia 30318-2112
www.peachtree-online.com

Text © 2005 by Steven Krasner
Illustration © 2005 by Keith Neely

Cover and book design by Melanie McMahon Ives

Manufactured in January 2010 in Harrisonburg, VA by R.R. Donnelley & Sons in the United States of America
10 9 8 7 6 5 4 3 2

Library of Congress Cataloging-in-Publication Data
Krasner, Steven.
  Play ball like the Hall of Famers / written by Steven Krasner ; illustrated by Keith Neely.-- 1st ed.
    p. cm.
  ISBN 978-1-56145-339-9 / 1-56145-339-0
  1. Baseball for children--Juvenile literature. 2. Baseball players--United States--Biography--Juvenile literature. I. Neely, Keith, 1943- ill. II. Title.
  GV880.4.K715 2005
  796.357'62--dc22
                               2004019836

For my Hall of Fame wife, Sue Oclassen

—S. K.

CONTENTS

★★★★★★★★★★★★★★★★★★★★★★★★★★★★★★

INTRODUCTION

★★★★★★★★★★★★★★★★★★★★★★★★★★★★★★

It takes many muscles, working in rhythm, to succeed in baseball.

A pitcher not only needs a strong arm, but also strong legs, in order to be effective on the mound. A hitter relies on his eyes, his hands, his arms, his hips and his legs to drive a baseball into the gap utilizing a nicely coordinated swing.

But there's another muscle that's just as important, if not more so.

The mind.

That muscle between the ears is often that which separates a good player from a great player. To make it into the Hall of Fame, a player has to be as strong mentally as he is physically gifted.

In this book, 19 Hall of Famers offer not only mechanical and technical tips that can make you a better ballplayer, but also insights into how mental preparation and focus can help you improve your overall abilities.

Every inning, every pitch is part of a game-long chess match in which out-thinking your opponent can pay dividends on the scoreboard.

Hitting, for example, can be broken down into the simple "see the ball, hit the ball" philosophy, and there's something to be said for that theory. But listen to Hall of Famers Rod Carew, Paul Molitor and George Brett. Their minds were racing as they dug into the batter's box.

How did the pitcher get me out last time? What pitch did he throw? What pitch should I expect him to throw this at-bat? A little knowledge can go a long way, giving you the best chance to succeed.

Similar mental exercises are performed all over the diamond, whether you're a power pitcher in the mold of a Tom Seaver and a Bob Feller, or a knuckleball specialist such as Phil Niekro, or a control artist such as Don Sutton.

Bunting. Hitting for power. Pickoff moves. Outfield play. Working behind the plate. Turning double plays. Running the bases. Stealing bases.

These are vital aspects of the game that take on added importance as you move up to the full-size diamond.

And who better to teach about these skills and the mental thought processes that augment these physical abilities than Hall of Famers?

Each chapter also includes the Hall of Famer's childhood baseball memories, his big-league memories, and any superstitions he may have had, in addition to a glossary of terms and a section called "The Mental Edge."

The players in this book were voted into the Hall of Fame by members of the Baseball Writers' Association of America. The yearly voting is very selective, generally resulting in only one or two players being inducted each year.

The National Baseball Hall of Fame and Museum is located in the picturesque village of Cooperstown, New York. Each player inducted is honored with a plaque that features his likeness and accomplishments, all of which dominate the Hall of Fame Gallery in the museum. The museum exhibits also feature artifacts and various topical displays covering all aspects of baseball history.

JOHNNY BENCH

Elected: 1989
Position: Catcher
Born: December 7, 1947, at Oklahoma City, Oklahoma
Height 6-1; Weight 210
Threw and batted right-handed

In Bench's first full season (1968), he won the National League's Rookie of the Year Award. As one of the leaders of Cincinnati's "Big Red Machine" teams of the 1970s, Bench was an outstanding, durable, defensive catcher. He won 10 consecutive Gold Gloves. He was equally impressive with a bat, belting 389 home runs. Bench earned two National League Most Valuable Player Awards.

As the pitch nears the plate, do you go out and get it or wait for it to come to you?

You want the ball to come to you.

There are certain times when the ball is getting into the strike zone or going down and out of the strike zone where it will get away from you and you have to reach for it, but for the most part you want the ball to come to you.

Why don't you want to reach for the pitch as a rule?

The ball gets to you faster than you can actually reach out, grab it, and pull it back. So the whole concept in catching is to sit back as comfortably as you can, with your arms relaxed and never stiff.

Is there one basic way to receive the ball?

The important thing is to catch every ball. There's not necessarily one way of doing it.

You want your catching position to be as natural and as comfortable as possible. Squat down the way that is easiest for you to squat. Don't worry about setting up high, and don't worry about getting your arms inside your knees. Be as comfortable as you possibly can and continue to practice as much as you can until you learn how to catch every ball.

How do you give a target?

You see some people with the glove up to give that great **target,** but the target should be given and then the hands should be relaxed so the arms can work in sequence, moving in an arc that can cover any area where the ball's thrown.

What does "framing pitches" mean?

Framing pitches means trying to make sure that when you catch the ball you give the impression that the ball is in the strike zone even if it's not, even if it's just off the plate.

How do you catch pitches so you're framing them?

You actually catch the ball in the web with a lot of the glove showing over the plate. The ball itself might be a couple of inches off the plate, but sometimes if you catch the ball this way you might be able to steal a strike call.

This is one of those times when you're reaching just a little for the ball because you have to go get the ball instead of catching it so far back. If the umpire can see the glove, he might react with the strike call.

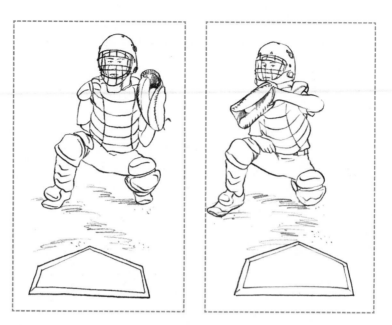

On a ball that's off to the side of the plate, you roll your hand over so the thumb and fingers are pointing out to the left or to the right. You receive the ball into the web, hoping that much of the glove is still covering the plate.

On a ball that's down, you turn your hand downward with your fingers pointing down so the web is down. Most of the glove, though, is still in the strike zone.

And of course, on the ball that's up in the strike zone, you're trying to catch the ball in the web with your fingers pointing up.

What are some of the major factors in deciding which pitches you might call for in a game?

You have to pay attention to and be comfortable with which pitches are working best for a pitcher on any particular day. Is the fastball moving, for instance? Is the pitcher able to change grips on the baseball to make the ball sink or run away or run in?

How important is it for the catcher to have the pitcher's trust?

The pitcher needs to have confidence in you and to know that the pitch you call is the right one.

You also have to work together throughout the game. For example, you may call for an inside pitch. You may want the fastball, but you want the sinking fastball, so you might have two different calls for the fastball. You need to have some kind of camaraderie with each pitcher so you can do that.

The best results come when a pitcher has complete faith in you, trusting that you understand what the pitches are going to be and that you know what **sequence** to use with the hitter.

What kind of location are you seeking from your pitcher?

For one thing, you want to throw first-pitch strikes, but that doesn't just mean thigh-high over the middle of the plate. That's a pitch any hitter likes.

I don't mean you can't throw a pitch over the middle of the plate. For instance, you may throw a sinker over the middle of the plate, but if it's down around the knees, there's nothing wrong with that location.

Do you want the pitcher to be hitting the corners of the plate all the time?

Some pitchers get so wound up trying to hit the corners that they end up missing, falling behind in the count, and getting so frustrated when they don't have their best control that they start aiming the ball. And when they do that, the ball isn't going to be moving in the strike zone. The ball is going to straighten out, and that pitcher's going to have a tough day.

How important is that movement in the strike zone?

If a pitcher is getting movement on the ball in the hitting area he's going to be much more successful.

How much effect on your signal-calling does the hitter have?

You have to have a sixth sense for what particular pitch the hitter might be looking for. So sequences can change throughout a game with a particular hitter.

6

What are you trying to do when you call a pitch?

The real idea is to try and get the hitter to swing at your pitch.

There are a lot of pitchers who say, "I've got this particular pitch and I'll challenge him right now and go right to it" rather than just working around and trying to make the hitter **chase** a pitch out of the zone.

But you want to call a pitch that allows the pitcher to throw to a weakness the hitter has, because every hitter has a tendency not to hit the ball as well in one area as he would in another.

In calling games, do you work around certain hitters?

There are certain hitters you're going to have much more success with than others. So you try to avoid the guy who's going to give you the most trouble.

Against him, you try to hit the corners of the plate. Sometimes you walk him. It's an unintentional walk, because you aren't standing outside and throwing the four traditional wide pitches. But you're trying to make that hitter chase a pitch, and if he decides to swing at a ball, then you've really put the percentages in your favor.

How much information can you learn about a hitter even before a game begins?

In the big leagues, there are scouting reports. Younger kids don't necessarily have those.

What you need to do is watch hitters in batting practice, see hitters' tendencies, check out their stances. Can they handle the inside pitch with that stance? Does this hitter **step in the bucket?** If so, he'll have trouble reaching the outside pitch, so that's what you might call for when he's up, have him chase the ball outside.

That's the sixth sense the good catchers have. That's how you learn to be a good caller of a game. You notice things about the batter, even as the game is going on.

How does a catcher run a game aside from pitch-calling?

A catcher needs to know what's going on all around the field.

If I knew there was a left-handed hitter who was a **dead pull hitter,** a few things would run through my mind. Can we pitch him away because he's going to try to pull it? Does the first baseman have to play deeper to guard the line? Do you shift the right side of the infield more toward right because he's likely to pull the ball? Do you move the left side of the infield?

You have to be aware of the outfielders' positioning. Let's say I'm going to try to pitch a particular hitter down and in with breaking balls and fastballs away. I have to figure out if I need the left fielder playing straightaway or toward the left field line. And because this particular hitter's tendency is to pull the ball on a breaking ball, there's a good chance a hit will be on the ground to the right side, so I know where I want my infielders playing.

I have to make sure the fielders are in the right positioning for the way we're pitching to this particular hitter. That's the way I have to approach it as the catcher.

What role does psychology play in the catcher's job?

There are several different types of pitcher mentalities and psyches that you have to take into account as a catcher.

Some guys need to be reassured, for instance. Some have to be told exactly what they need to do and have everything programmed.

First there's the pitcher you're very comfortable with. All you have to do with him is make sure he's on track mechanically, maybe make sure he has his motion right, remind him to stay back in his delivery or keep his arm on top or take a deep breath. Or you might pace a pitcher by fixing the dirt in the batter's box and controlling how fast you work behind the plate.

And then there's the guy you really have to get on. He might be a little lazy. He might let his concentration slip. So sometimes you have to emphasize with a little bit of authority that he's not doing it mechanically the way he should.

How do you deal with these different personalities and mentalities?

Say you need the pitcher to give you a certain pitch.

With one guy you might go out there and say, "Look, here's the situation. Here's a batter who's going to pull the ball, so make sure you get over to cover first base on a ground ball hit to the right side." Or, you tell him, "Here's a batter we're not going to let beat us. Don't aim it. Let me have breaking balls down on the outside corner."

With other guys you go out to the mound to talk to him so you can calm him down. Maybe you just want to make him aware of the situation that has come up in a game, to make sure you slow him down at times because you see that he has become frustrated with what has been going on. And you remind him how he needs to approach the game at that point.

Depending on the pitcher and the situation you might say, "Everything's going to be fine, just take a deep breath, get after it right here, and let's get the situation in hand."

What's the bottom line for a catcher as psychologist?

You've got to be able to understand all of your pitchers. As a catcher, I have to bring each pitcher to the highest level he can reach.

How important are the legs for a catcher?

You have to work hard and get your legs in the best shape, almost stronger than they need to be. Guys get strong in their upper body, and you want your arms strong. But the legs are the real key. You've got to block the plate. You've got to withstand people trying to knock you over at the plate, and you've got to come out of your crouch to throw. So there's a great deal of strength needed in the legs.

How can a catcher have a good game?

There are four ways a catcher can have a good game to contribute to the team. The first priority is to call a good game, especially when you need to help a pitcher who maybe doesn't have his good stuff that day. A catcher can throw out runners. He can block home plate. And he can hit.

How important is it for a catcher to be able to separate his offensive and defensive responsibilities?

You have to be able to do that. There are some guys who might put down the signals for a fastball or a curveball, but they're really not thinking about the situation in the game and what might be the best pitch at that point. They may be thinking about offense, maybe a tough at-bat they just had.

If you lose your concentration and don't focus on what's happening right now, it could put the pitcher and the team in a tough spot.

As a catcher, how difficult is it to concentrate on hitting when it's your turn to hit?

You really have trouble doing that. Maybe the first time up it's all right, but you're still worried about your pitcher and calling a good game.

There are so many variables that go into concentration. There are certain days when your best pitcher is out there throwing—like (Hall of Famer) Tom Seaver, for instance—and then you don't have to worry quite as much behind the plate. But then you have pitchers who make you have to work a little harder. You know it's a day when you're going to have to score a lot of runs to win.

When it's time for you to hit, maybe there's a pitcher out there you pretty much own, someone you've had great success against in the past. Or maybe it's a guy who gives you a lot of trouble. So you have to concentrate on hitting. That usually happens when you take your bat out of the rack and go to the **on-deck circle.** But even when you're getting your bat and getting ready to hit, there are times when the pitching coach or the manager will come to you and want to know something about your pitcher.

There's a lot going on for a catcher. But if a player can't handle all of it, then put him at first base or in the outfield.

★ ★ ★ YOUTH BASEBALL MEMORIES ★ ★ ★

I played Home Run Derby all the time. I learned to try to hit the ball out of the ballpark. I grew up in such a small town (Binger, Oklahoma) that there weren't a lot of other kids around. There were three kids I grew up with and played ball with. We made up games. Some people had Wiffle balls, but the point of the games was always to see how far you could hit the ball.

When I was 14, I was playing American Legion baseball with 17- and 18-year-olds. Back in those days you always felt bad if you didn't get two or three hits a game.

We won the state championship. I actually pitched the six games of the finals of each tournament, the county and district tournaments. I had a heck of a curve. I threw a big curveball from different angles. I could make guys' knees break with my curveball. How hard could I throw the ball? Over the plate.

I hit .633 my senior year in high school (Binger High), so I don't feel like anyone looked at me as a pitcher. They liked my offense a little more because I had power and I could catch, although no one saw me catch much.

I pitched a lot, and we had another kid who caught who wouldn't play third, so I played third base too. And when I played American Legion baseball, they already had catchers, so I had to go to another town and I played a lot of first base. It was either play first base or sit on the bench. The last year I finally got to catch.

★ ★ ★ BIG-LEAGUE MEMORIES ★ ★ ★

Winning the World Championship (in 1975 and 1976) is probably my biggest memory. But almost every time we went out on the field was a special moment during our days as the Big Red Machine.

I remember playing in the 1969 All-Star Game in Washington and hitting a home run off Mel Stottlemyre my first at-bat. I hit it very deep to left, where they had a high wall. That highlight actually came during my two weeks of summer camp in the Army. Our camp was in Virginia, not far from Washington, and they let me off from duty to play in the game.

My first year (1968), I went to the All-Star Game in Houston. I was picked as catcher. Willie Mays came over to me in the clubhouse before the game and said, "You should be the starting catcher." That was one huge highlight, that he would say that to me. Jerry Grote was the starting catcher, but they let me catch the ninth inning.

There were other highlights, like the home run I hit off Pittsburgh's Dave Giusti to tie the game in the playoffs in 1972. I led off the ninth with a home run. Then, of course, there was hitting two home runs against the Yankees in the fourth game of the 1976 World Series and being MVP of that series.

★★★ SUPERSTITIONS ★★★

I had no superstitions as a player.

Did I throw with the same guy every day? No. Did I wear the same sweat-shirt every day? No. If I were on a hot streak I might reach into the locker and grab the sweatshirt I wore the day before, but as temperatures change, so does the uniform. I might not even need a sweatshirt the next day.

MENTAL EDGE

When a game is over, no one on the field is likely to be more exhausted than the catcher. The mental exhaustion will be just as great, if not greater, than the physical exhaustion.

As the game wears on, sweat is pouring down his face and arms, his leg muscles are fatigued from the up-and-down squatting nature of the position. His arm muscles are tired from all of the throws back to the pitcher, not to mention any throws trying to gun down base-stealers. His body is bruised from foul tips and pitches thrown in the dirt. The sweat-soaked equipment seems to weigh twice as much as it did when the first pitch was delivered.

But despite all of that, the catcher has to stay sharp mentally. The catcher's concentration can't waver. He keeps thinking.

How strong is my pitcher? What pitch is his best one today? What should I call in a certain situation? What is the umpire's strike zone on this particular day? What do I see the batter doing in the box, possibly giving away his approach to the next pitch? Is the runner at first looking to steal second? Does my pitcher need a breather? Should I go out and talk to him? What should I say? Should I bark at him, sternly telling him to bear down because I sense he's losing his concentration? Should I crack a joke to get him to loosen up because it's a pressure situation and he's too tense?

The catcher's mind, and body, cannot rest at any point in the game.

—*S. K.*

GLOSSARY

Chase: To go after a pitch out of the strike zone.

Dead Pull Hitter: A right-handed hitter who generally hits the ball to the left side of the field; a left-handed hitter who generally hits the ball to the right side of the field.

On-Deck Circle: The place on the field between the plate and the dugout where the next hitter waits his turn to go to the plate.

Sequence: The order in which signals are given.

Step in the Bucket: When the batter's front foot moves away from the plate, toward the foul line, as the pitch comes in and he begins to swing.

Target: Where you want to throw the ball. For a pitcher, the target is where the catcher holds up his mitt.

★★★★★★★★★★★★★★★★★★★★★★★★★★★★

GEORGE BRETT

★★★★★★★★★★★★★★★★★★★★★★★★★★★★

Elected: 1999
Position: Third base
Born: May 15, 1953, at Glen Dale,
  West Virginia
Height 6-0; Weight 200
Threw right-handed, batted left-handed

George Brett spent his entire 21-year career with the Kansas City Royals, tormenting American League pitchers. An intense competitor, the 12-time All-Star became the only player in history to amass more than 3,000 hits, 300 homers, 600 doubles, 100 triples, and 200 stolen bases. The only player to win batting titles in three decades (1976, 1980, 1990), he was the American League's Most Valuable Player in 1980 when his remarkable .390 average was the highest since Ted Williams's .406 mark in 1941.

What's the best batting stance?

There are 650 different players in the Major Leagues, and 650 different stances. They are all correct for the different players.

To emulate a Major League player is probably not a bad way to go as you get older, but you also have to realize you will make changes in your stance as you progress.

Did you make changes?

I first copied Carl Yastrzemski. He was a left-handed hitter like I was, and he used to hold his bat straight up high and his left shoulder up with a little wiggle as he got ready.

That stance worked for me in high school, and it worked for me a little in Rookie League ball. It didn't work as much for me in Class A through Triple A, and it sure as heck didn't work for me in the Major Leagues, so I had to change my stance to give myself a better chance of being successful.

What's the possible drawback of a youngster copying a big-leaguer's stance?

It irritates me sometimes to see kids maybe 8 to 11 years old trying to copy guys in the majors who have worked on their stances for years and years. Kids at 8 or 9 aren't quick enough to hit like Jeff Bagwell does or strong enough to wiggle the bat like Gary Sheffield does and be successful.

Are there some basics kids should know about a stance?

The ideal stance is somewhere where the bat is parallel or up to a 45-degree angle to the ground, with the bat coming through the **hitting zone** level to the ground with a slight up swing.

If the bat starts pretty much on the same plane as your swing, fewer things can go wrong. You will have a less mechanical, more fluid swing.

If you hold the bat sticking high up in the air, a lot of things can go wrong mechanically. You can develop a big loop to your swing, especially when young, instead of taking a straighter line to the ball.

Are loops necessarily bad in a swing?

Loops aren't bad. A lot of people swing with loops. But a looping swing makes the swing longer, and to me, the shorter the swing, the better hitter you're going to be.

How should you start a swing?

I'm a firm believer in rhythm. Don't stand at the plate flat-footed. Wiggle the bat back and forth. Keep moving a bit to keep the tension out of your hands, arms, and legs.

When are you moving like this?

When the pitcher is getting ready to throw, while he's looking in for the **sign.** You don't want to be standing still. If the pitcher takes a while to get the sign and throw, that means you're waiting at the plate for a long time. After a while like that, you see batters call time out.

The only time that should happen is if a pitcher is holding a runner on. You're in the box, and you keep on thinking he's going to throw the ball to home plate and he's holding the ball. Then you start feeling tension building up in your legs and arms. You don't want tension.

Why don't you want tension?

Charley Lau, my batting coach with the Royals, used to use the word "cancer" when he used the word "tension." Tension can kill your swing because you're not fluid, which means you're not able to be quick with your swing. Tension slows everything down because you're grabbing the bat too hard.

I see so many guys gripping the bat too tightly. They grab it like they're strangling somebody.

How tightly do you want to grip the bat?

Holding the bat was explained to me at a very early age, and I think that's why I was somewhat successful: You want to grip the bat with the same amount of pressure as you would a tube of toothpaste held upside down with the lid off and you don't want any of it to come out.

It's the same as in golf. Golfers don't put the death grip on their clubs. They go up there and just barely hold onto the club. At the point of contact, yeah, they tighten up. It's the same with swinging a baseball bat.

It's amazing to me how many players have too much tension in their swing. They're up there trying to hit the ball a mile, and they're gripping the bat so tightly that it takes away the fluidity of the swing.

I've always said that when you hit a ball well, the swing seems almost effortless. And when you don't have tension in your body, it feels a lot more effortless.

What's the best recipe for hitting for power?

Hitting for power comes from your rhythm, your **extension** through the ball on your swing, and your weight shift. What I mean by the weight shift is the transfer of your weight from the back leg when you start your swing to the front leg as you swing. And as you hit the ball, you extend your arms through the swing.

Does every power hitter have to follow the same method?

There are some guys who are big enough and strong enough that they don't have to rely on that fluid swing on a daily basis to hit home runs.

If you're not the biggest kid on the block, can you still hit for power?

I wasn't the biggest and strongest. There are those hitters like myself who needed a good weight shift from a firm back side to the front side. If I didn't do that, I wouldn't have hit so many home runs—no ifs, ands, or buts about it.

Again, it's the same with golfers. When the golfer takes his club back, where does his weight go? It goes back. When he swings and makes contact with the ball, where does his weight end up? On the forward leg.

In baseball, you keep that little rhythm going—the pitcher gets ready to throw, you start leaning back, you get your weight on your back side, the ball comes, you move forward, you make contact, you swing through the ball, your arms are extended. And now where's your weight? On the front side.

How important are the legs in the swing?

What muscles are stronger, your legs or your arms? Your legs are stronger than your arms. So use them. And if you don't get your weight back before you come forward in your swing, guess what? You're swinging all upper body, all upper torso, and you won't be able to drive the ball as far as you would if you had a good weight transfer.

What's the best advice for coming through in clutch situations?

Try easier, not harder.

The more pressure you put on yourself, the harder the task is going to be. So, try easier, not harder. That's my theory.

What about the pressure on the hitter in those situations?

The pressure is more on the pitcher than it is on the hitter.

A hitter who fails 7 times out of 10 still hits .300, which is a good average. But a pitcher who fails 7 out of 10 times, isn't going to be pitching in key situations for very long.

Again, try easier, not harder. If you try too hard, that's when you get tension, which you don't want.

What role does confidence play in becoming a good clutch hitter?

Obviously, you need confidence that you're able to do the job. You have to want to be the guy in the clutch situation. "Okay, I'm the right guy. I can do this." I always thought I was a better hitter than the guy I was facing was a pitcher, regardless of whom I was facing.

You pump yourself up, rather than saying, "I hope the guy before me comes through because I don't want to hit in this situation." You never want to think like that.

It's difficult to go up there and compete in the clutch until you've had some success in the late innings helping your ballclub win. The more you've done it, the more confidence you'll have. If you have a lot of confidence it makes your job a lot easier. Then you're able to control your emotions better.

How were you able to control your emotions in clutch at-bats?

I would always make sure I was breathing properly.

I would take a lot of deep breaths because that relaxes you, and I always tried to have a smile on my face. When you smile, it relaxes you. I'd try to downplay the situation. You build yourself up. You tell yourself that this pitcher does not want to face you.

And the more you believe in that, the easier it is to convince yourself, and the more success you're going to have.

Do you become more aggressive when you're hitting in a key situation?

That depends on who's hitting behind you and who's pitching. If I were facing Goose Gossage, for instance, and I had Amos Otis hitting behind me, I would sure as heck want to face Goose Gossage and swing at a ball that was two inches out of the strike zone rather than have Amos Otis hitting against him because Amos didn't like facing him.

Why do left-handed hitters seem to have more trouble hitting left-handed pitchers than the righty-righty matchups?

It's probably more difficult for left-handed hitters because they don't face many left-handed pitchers when they're growing up.

What was your plan for having success against left-handers?

I just tried to hit the ball up the middle against them. That way, if you tried to hit the ball up the middle, you wouldn't get tricked on breaking balls over the outside corner as often. You'll be waiting on the ball a little longer.

What can happen if you try to pull left-handers?

If you go up there as a left-handed hitter and try to **pull** the ball on a regular basis, and you don't see left-handers that often, you're going to get fooled on breaking balls. Of the breaking balls left-handers throw, 99 percent of them are away. So if you're trying to pull, you won't be able to reach those balls, or if you do, you won't be able to **drive** the ball. That's why hitting to the opposite field is the easiest plan.

So what I tried to do against left-handers, especially with two strikes, was think more about hitting the ball the opposite way. If I did that, I could still react to a good fastball in and still get my bat around on it. Looking to hit to the opposite field helped me keep my front shoulder in, which is a key for left-handed batters hitting against left-handed pitchers.

★★★ YOUTH BASEBALL MEMORIES ★★★

I remember when I was 17 and 18 years old, playing shortstop for El Segundo High School, we played for the state championship for Southern California in Anaheim Stadium in front of 25,000 people. That's kind of an adrenaline rush. We lost to Lompoc High School in my junior year and then beat the same team to win the state championship my senior year.

My high school team had two first-round picks on it: Roy Thomas was a pitcher, and Roy Howell was the third baseman. I was a second-round pick. We had Scott MacGregor (a left-hander who starred for the Baltimore Orioles) on our team. He pitched my junior and senior years.

We played 100 games a year, so it's hard for particular games or performances to stand out. We played 40 games my senior year. We entered four tournaments with maybe 25 to 30 teams in each of them, with double elimination. As soon as the regular season ended we'd go right into American Legion ball where we would play another 60 games. They all kind of run together.

★★★ BIG-LEAGUE MEMORIES ★★★

Obviously winning the 1985 World Series is one of my biggest memories. We came back from behind, three games to one, in the American League playoffs, and we came back from behind, three games to one, in the World Series, so we had to win the last three games to win the Series (over the St. Louis Cardinals), which we did. That was a big thrill.

I remember in 1980 hitting a home run off the Yankees' Goose Gossage to win the third and final game of the playoffs in New York. At the time we were losing, and I hit a two-run homer late in the game to give us the lead and we held on.

In 1976 I hit a three-run homer in the eighth inning off the Yankees' Grant Jackson to tie it in the last game of the playoff series, but Chris

Chambliss hit the home run in the bottom of the ninth that beat us in the fifth and final game.

I remember my 3,000th hit. It was off Tim Fortugno, a left-handed reliever for the Angels. That culminated a 4-for-5 game. I had gotten hits in my first three at-bats in Anaheim Stadium, the same place I played my high school state championship games. There were a lot of people from Kansas City who came out to the series in anticipation of my reaching that milestone. I didn't play the first two games of the series because I had a pulled muscle in my shoulder and was really sore.

That was pretty special, not only getting 3,000 hits but because of where I got the 3,000th. A lot of the Southern California friends I grew up with were at the game. I also had a lot of friends and family from Kansas City there. And my brother, Ken, was an announcer for the Angels at that time. So he basically called it, which was kind of cool.

There are a ton of memories: losing in the 1976 playoffs, the 1977 playoffs, the 1978 playoffs, the 1980 World Series, the 1981 playoffs, the 1984 playoffs—then winning it all in 1985. Even those times when you've lost and you don't think you'll ever regroup, you look back at them now and you smile and say, that was so much fun, competing at that level. Everything just seemed so important, and you were part of it, part of baseball, part of the history of the game.

★★★ SUPERSTITIONS ★★★

None. I didn't have any. I wasn't smart enough to have superstitions because I couldn't remember from one day to the next what I did.

MENTAL EDGE

The game is on the line.

The bases are loaded. It's the bottom of the last inning. There are two outs. The opposition's best relief pitcher is on the mound. A base hit wins the game.

The fans are roaring. Teammates are yelling out encouragement as the batter strolls to the plate.

The batter is well aware of the pressure. If he gets a base hit, he's a hero. If he makes an out, he has failed to come through in the clutch for his team. There is no middle ground. Hero or goat. That about sums it up.

But the batter knows he can't get consumed by the pressure. He has to realize that there's just as much pressure, if not more, on the pitcher. The pitcher has to throw strikes, quality strikes, not just pitches down the middle of the plate. There's little margin for error on his part.

The batter understands this. Still, he feels the heat. But as he settles into the batter's box for the first pitch of this critical at-bat, he takes a deep breath. He tells himself to relax. He tells himself he can come through in this situation. He's done it before, he can do it again.

Then he looks out at the pitcher. He's relaxed. He's confident. He's ready.

Neither he, nor his teammates, can ask for anything more.

—*S. K.*

23

GLOSSARY

Drive: To hit the ball with authority.

Extension: The follow-through with the swing, as far as possible.

Hitting zone: The area at the plate where the ball arrives from the pitcher, generally the strike zone.

Pull: For a right-handed hitter, it's hitting the ball to the left side of the field; for a left-handed hitter, it's hitting hit the ball to the right side of the field.

Sign: The pitch-selection signal from the catcher.

ROD CAREW

Elected: 1991
Position: Second base
Born: October 1, 1945, at Gatun, Panama
Height 6-0; Weight 182
Threw right-handed, batted left-handed

National Baseball Hall of Fame Library, Cooperstown, NY

Rod Carew lined, chopped, and bunted his way to 3,053 career hits. He captured seven batting titles. He used a variety of relaxed, crouched batting stances to hit over .300 in 15 consecutive seasons with the Twins and Angels, achieving a .328 lifetime batting average. He was the American League's Rookie of the Year in 1967, and he won the league's Most Valuable Player Award in 1977. He was named to 18 consecutive All-Star teams.

As a left-handed hitter, how do you bunt for a hit?

One of the keys that I try to teach is to bring the back (left) leg up and cross it over in front of the front (right) leg, which you slide open just a little bit like you're taking a short walking step toward the pitcher. You step toward the pitcher. You don't pull your body weight toward the first-base line with this crossover step.

Most kids, when they're bunting from the left side, want to start moving toward first base before they make contact with the ball. If you do that, you will

have a tendency to foul the ball off because you're reaching for the ball as you're moving away from it, down the first-base line.

Why take a crossover step?

That step will keep your body in line to the pitcher. And it will give you some momentum after you drop the bunt down. You're also still in position to cover the entire plate width with your bat.

Where is your bat when you're taking this crossover step?

You want to have the bat out in front of you; as I start my crossover step I also start taking the bat cut, holding it up, at a 45-degree angle. You want to try to bunt the ball down toward the end of the bat, and you want to keep your hands loose on the bat, because that way it will **deaden** the ball coming off the bat.

Why keep the bat at a 45-degree angle?

If the pitch is up in the strike zone, that's a good angle to cover the ball with your bat, and you can get the ball down easily.

What if the pitch was down in the strike zone?

You still want to have a good angle with the bat. A lot of times when the ball is down in the zone, the hitter will have a tendency to just drop the **bat head** to the ball. If he does that, he'll be likely to foul the ball off.

What you want to do on a ball that's down is to flex your knees and go down to the ball with your body, keeping a good angle for bunting with your bat instead of reaching down and just dropping the bat head to the ball. You should always have some flexibility in your legs when you have to go down to get a ball and put it in play.

Should you bunt the ball to third base, or drag it to the right side?

I have always felt that third base is the best place to bunt the ball because when you bunt the ball down the third-base line, you don't have to be perfect with it.

Why doesn't it have to be perfect?

Wherever you bunt the ball down the line, the third baseman is going to have to charge in, field the ball, and make a throw to first. When he makes that throw, the chances are he's going to be off-balance, and that can help you beat the bunt out for a hit. It's not very comfortable for any third baseman to come running in, scoop up the ball, and throw off-balance all in one motion.

What if the third baseman was playing in, expecting the bunt?

I didn't care where he was playing. I had a mental spot, where I wanted the ball to go and stop, and I worked on getting the ball to stop in that spot. I knew if I hit that spot 8 out of 10 times, I had a great chance of getting a base hit.

But what if you get thrown out? Would that stop you from bunting?

If I missed my spot and the third baseman came in and made a heckuva play and got me out, I challenged him again. Kids today don't want to do that. They'll put a bunt down and get thrown out, and they won't want to try it again. You have to keep working at it. Keep trying him again and again.

How does bunting a lot to third help you out at the plate?

It does more than just get you base hits on the bunt itself. If you draw the third baseman in because he's expecting you to bunt, you can hit balls past him that he would have gotten had he been playing back in his normal position. If he's in, he can't react as well to those balls. That's why bunting to third can be such an effective weapon, in more ways than one.

What about bunting to the right side? Why does that have to be a more perfect bunt?

When you **drag** a bunt to that side of the diamond, it has to be perfect because there's a little "triangle" on the field over there between the pitcher, the second baseman, and the first baseman. If you don't put the bunt down in that little "triangle," it's easy for one of those fielders to make a play on the bunt. That's like a wasted at-bat because you will be out.

When you're hitting, how important is the stride as part of the mechanics?

To me, a **stride** is overrated. You can stride, but you don't necessarily have to. You can just stand at the plate and use your hands and your hips: fire your hands at the ball and rotate your hips through the hitting zone. If you do that, you can still hit the ball nine miles, even without a long stride.

What are the advantages of a short stride?

I took a short stride because I wanted to make sure that when I did stride, my body was centered as I hit the ball. I never wanted to be out on my front foot too much, and I didn't want to be too far back on my back side when I started swinging at a pitch.

Are you standing still when the pitch comes in and you begin to swing?

No, you have to get back, rock your body back into what I call the launch position. You start everything in the beginning of your swing mechanics back, and then you go forward.

And when you take your stride forward, when your front foot hits the ground, if you stopped the action, you should be able to take an imaginary pole and it should be able to come straight down the hitter's body. You want that balance as you get ready to hit the ball.

What happens after the front foot comes down?

The next things that fire out in your swing are your hands and your hips.

How do you teach this method?

When I work with young hitters, I don't allow them to stride at first. If I'm **soft-tossing** with them, I flip them the ball, and as I do that, I have them take their hands back and then start their hands toward the ball and rotate their hips at the same time.

Doing that gives them the feeling of that vertical pole, balanced position that they should be hitting from. Then, gradually, I get them to stride into the ball, putting it all together.

What happens if a stride is too long?

Overstriding causes the bat to travel a long distance through the hitting zone and your swing won't be as compact as it should be. If your stride is too long, you'll start dragging the bat through the zone and you won't be as consistently successful.

Why not?

Dragging the bat through the zone gives you slower **bat speed.**

If you fly open too quickly—that is, if you start your swing too soon or if you're overstriding and you get out on your front foot—your hands are coming from behind you to get the bat to the ball.

Your hips will already be opened up, so your hands have a longer distance to travel to the baseball. That creates a loop in your swing. It's more difficult to be a consistent hitter if you have a loop in your swing.

Shouldn't the hips open up before your hands come through the zone?

That's a theory some people have, but I don't like the theory of hips first and then the hands follow.

Why not?

I had success the other way. I would start my hands first and let my hips follow. To me, if you start your hips first, your hands are going to drag through the zone. If I started my hands first and let my hips follow, my hands were going to go in a straight line to the ball, which is what I wanted them to do.

Does it matter if you're a power hitter or a hitter who puts the ball in play with singles and doubles?

I don't think it matters what type of hitter you are.

To me, if you're a power hitter and you fly open too soon, you're not only going to be relying on strictly your upper body for whatever power you can get into the ball, but you also can be pitched to more easily.

What do you mean by that?

If a pitcher is smart and he knows you're going to fly open too soon, why throw a pitch on the inside of the plate? Why not just throw pitches to the outside part of the plate? Because if you're flying open too soon, you can't cover the outside part of the plate with your bat. You won't do too much damage to a pitch on the outside of the plate.

Can there be success in hitting the ball to the opposite field?

Some people would say charts show that your batting average goes down if you consistently hit the outside pitch, but I never believed that. I was a left-handed hitter and I wore out the left-field line and left-center.

How did you do that?

The big thing is to track the ball. Don't try and guess what the pitch will be. Follow the pitch out of the pitcher's hand to see what it's doing. You only have a split-second to see the ball.

Why is that important?

The baseball actually dictates to you as a hitter where you should hit it. You don't dictate what you're going to do with the pitch. The baseball tells you.

If the pitch is inside, the ball tells me I have a couple of choices. I can **pull** the ball, I can hit it up the middle, or I can give it an inside-out swing and, as a left-handed hitter, take the ball to left.

If the ball is on the outside part of the plate, it's telling me I better hit this ball to the **opposite field** because if I try to pull this pitch, I'm going to **roll over** on it and, as a left-handed hitter, hit a weak ground ball to the right side.

What's the best method for hitting to the opposite field?

A lot of people teach that you should let the ball get deep into the hitting zone before you swing to hit to the opposite field. You can do that, but if you do, there's a good chance of fouling that pitch off if the timing isn't just right.

So what I tried to do was to have my weight forward a little bit, but at the same time I would get my hands out so my bat would still be in fair territory when I hit the ball. I'd drop the bat head a bit and slice the ball into fair territory.

How important is it to have the mindset that you want to hit the ball to the opposite field?

It's important. Hitters don't often think that way. They get into one frame of thought, which is trying to pull everything. That's why you don't see consistency in hitters.

What type of swing is best?

I try to teach kids to stay on top of the ball, to hit the top half of the ball as much as possible.

Why?

I want them to get the feeling of always hitting the ball, making contact. The more you stay on top of the ball, the more line drives you're going to hit and the better hitter you'll become. You want that consistency instead of trying to uppercut the ball all the time. If you try to uppercut the ball and hit

it high in the air, you have more of a tendency to foul off pitches. And the more you swing up, the more your head is going to come off the ball.

Why is that a problem?

You want to see the ball hit the bat. The head is very important. You have to try and keep your head as still as possible.

What are some tips for hitting left-handed pitchers as a left-handed batter?

When you watch left-handers hit against left-handed pitchers, they always seem to want to swing up on the ball. And a lot of times when they're swinging up, they're also **bailing** out of the batter's box, pulling off the baseball.

I believe if more left-handers tried to stay on top of the ball when they batted against left-handers, they would be able to stay in the box longer.

How does that help them?

It will keep their front shoulder in better. If they start to pull off the ball, the front side goes off, too, and you can't see the ball as well and you don't have the plate coverage you need. It's still, though, all about tracking the ball, seeing what the ball is doing, and having the kind of swing you feel comfortable with, a swing you know will allow you to make contact.

What did you want to remember about each at-bat?

What did the pitcher get me out on? What did he start me off with? What was his second pitch? I kept notes when I faced a guy. And I'd go back over those notes when I faced that pitcher again because we didn't have a video system. Keeping notes is how I learned about the pitchers in the league. If I knew what he might throw to me, I could be ready for it the next time and become a better hitter.

What were some of the things you looked for when you studied a pitcher?

If a kid is a two-pitch pitcher (fastball, breaking ball), I tell the batters to look for the fastball because that's the pitch kids hit best. That's the pitch that every big league ballplayer hits best.

Some guys might go up to the plate looking for change-ups and breaking balls. But if they're looking for the change-up or the curveball, and the pitcher throws a fastball, they'll be late with their swing and won't hit the ball well if they hit it at all.

You're never going to be late if you look for the fastball. You adjust down to the change-up and the breaking balls, keeping your hands back. It's harder to adjust up to a fastball.

How tightly should you grip the bat?

Everyone has different theories about that. I held my bat very loosely in my hands because I felt if my hands were loose on the bat, my whole body would be loose. If I started squeezing sawdust out of the bat, that meant I was all tense, and I never wanted to have that feeling of tension at the plate. I wanted to be relaxed.

My hands were loose as I got back into my launch position, which was taking my hands back. When I got ready to explode to the ball with the momentum and bat speed that the launch position helped to generate, that's when I started squeezing the bat.

As a base-stealer, how important is having great speed?

It's great to have sheer speed, but knowledge of what the pitchers do is very important.

What do you look for?

You look for what kind of tendencies they have. You try to pick up things like, does he leave his front (left) shoulder open if he's a right-handed pitcher in his set position?

If he does, then as soon as he closes that shoulder, meaning he brings it back toward home plate in his motion, in that split-second when he's closing that shoulder you can get a good jump toward second base because once he closes that shoulder toward home plate, he can't throw over to first. That would be a **balk,** and you would be given second base, as the runner.

Some people say you should look to see if the right-handed pitcher is collapsing on his back leg, that is, getting in position to push off the rubber, which would mean he was going to throw to the plate and not to first base. But to me the guy's biggest giveaway was his front shoulder.

What else do you want to know about the pitcher?

You want to know what the pitcher likes to throw in certain situations.

Why is that important?

It helps if you can pick a time when he's going to throw a breaking ball. If he's throwing a breaking ball, you have a much better chance of stealing a base because the pitch is going to get to home plate at a slower rate of speed than a fastball would.

As a base-stealer trying to steal second, what was your first step?

You hear a lot that you should cross over, that your first step should be with the left foot, crossing over the right foot. I had a tendency to first slide my front (right) foot open (from a position facing in toward the infield to a position facing second base). That was my first quick move; then I could cross over.

How did this help you?

It put my body in a position to run in a straight line toward second base. Plus, it also gave me some leverage to open up and push off and go. To me, keeping the front foot closed and then crossing over wasn't a comfortable position. I would slide that front foot, and when I crossed over, I was already open and ready to go.

What was your body position when you took off?

The first couple of steps I tried to stay low. A lot of kids take that first step and then pop up. They don't realize they're slowing themselves down. If they can learn to stay down the first two or three steps I think that will be a lot better.

When you're running to steal a base, would you look back at the hitter?

The only time you look back at the hitter is on a hit-and-run play. To me, when you're stealing from first base, your objective is to get to second base. You can't worry about what's going on at home plate. If the batter hits a line drive directly at someone and it turns into a double play, there's nothing you can do about it.

You see a lot of runners wanting to peek. When they peek back at the hitter, though, they slow themselves down.

How do you take your lead?

Everything is done from a balanced position. Hitting is from a balanced position, pitching is from a balanced position, fielding ground balls is from a balanced position, and it's the same with baserunning.

Your body is centered when you've taken your lead. You're not leaning to go to the next base. You're not leaning back to your starting base. You're not on your toes, but on the balls of your feet. You don't want to be flat-footed. As the front foot turns, you get on the ball of your back foot and push off with that foot.

Does your base-stealing lead change depending on what base you're on?

It's a little different.

When you're stealing second base, you might get a bit of a **walking lead** off the bag. There's someone holding you on at first base, so you can't get too far off. Sometimes the pitcher will hold the ball and make you come to a stop. You don't want to start too soon and get picked off.

Some guys like to start closer to the bag with their lead. That way as the pitcher is going into his windup the runner can have more of a walking lead, a **secondary lead** that can give him momentum toward second base, instead of going from a standstill.

Trying to steal third base, you take your lead, and then there's a secondary lead. No one is holding you on at second base like they do at first base. The second baseman or the shortstop will try to keep you close, but it's different. So my first lead might be just a couple of steps off the bag, and for my secondary lead, I go a few steps farther as the pitcher is beginning his motion.

How do you get back to the bag when the pitcher throws over?

I always went back with my foot first. I never went back headfirst because I didn't want anything happening to my hands. My hands were very important to my hitting, so I didn't want anyone stepping on my hands.

Over time you know how far off you are and how long it will take you to get back to the bag.

Left-handers are tougher to steal second base on because they're facing the hitter in their stretch position. How did you steal against lefties?

Some left-handers would give away when they were coming over. Some of them would look at first base when they were going to throw a pitch to the plate, and then they would look toward home when they were going to throw over, trying to trick you.

What did you look for?

I used to look at their leg kick. If it was straight up and down, it was tougher to get a good jump. If they happened to kick that (right) leg back a bit, then I knew I could run because after bringing that leg back, it would be a balk if they then threw over to first base. If the leg kick was straight up and down, you had to be careful because from that position the pitcher could still legally either go to home plate or come over with a throw.

Some runners will take off on the left-hander's first move, whether he's going to the plate or back to first base. Did you?

You can do that, but I never liked going on first move because I hated getting picked off. And if his first move was to first base, you'd be picked off. To me it was embarrassing to get picked off. I wanted to be absolutely sure I saw something in his move I could take advantage of in stealing a base.

How did you try to do that?

At times I would take a longer lead at first base than normal, just to get the pitcher to throw over to first base a few times. That way I could read what he was doing.

★★★ YOUTH BASEBALL MEMORIES ★★★

I grew up in Panama. When I was 13, I was playing with kids who were 20 or 21 years old, because I was that much advanced in baseball.

It was always something that was easy for me. It was fun for me because I was an abused child. I was abused by my dad. And baseball took me away from home and made me feel like I was Superman. I blocked out everything else when I was playing baseball. Baseball was my outlet to get me away.

I felt I was so much more in command of baseball skills than the other kids. I could always hit. I could run. I could steal bases. I needed work on my fielding, but baseball came easy to me. I was blessed. God gave me a talent that many youngsters would like to have, but in addition to that blessing, I also worked hard. I didn't just take my ability for granted. I worked at improving my skills day in and day out.

We had to make our own bats, so we used to take broomsticks and turn them into bats. Sometimes we used bottle caps as baseballs. We'd fill them with mud for fastballs, and we'd use empty bottle caps to glide through the air and try to hit them as they floated all around.

We didn't have a lot of equipment. We made our own baseballs out of newspaper and string. For gloves we'd take canvas, draw fingers on it, and then cut out two pieces and sew them together.

When I was growing up this is what we did because we wanted to play. So we went out and played. In Latin America, that's how it is. You play every day.

We didn't have the best fields. We played on fields where we needed cranes to dig up some of the boulders that were out there. But it got better. When I was growing up the fields were bad, with a lot of rocks. Then my uncle, who was in charge of the physical education program, started to clean up the fields and make them better for us to play on.

When I was 13 or 14 we had organized teams. We had a good organized Little League program.

I played shortstop and pitched. I didn't like pitching. I **drilled** a kid one time, and I was the hardest thrower on the team. I didn't like pitching after that because I felt like I hurt him. I told the manager I didn't want to pitch anymore and to put me back at shortstop.

I was a power hitter when I was a kid. I changed my whole way of hitting when I got into pro ball. I think in Little League I hit something like .675. I remember getting a Ted Williams bat for being the Most Valuable Player. I later told Ted Williams that was the first real bat I ever had. The first time I met him was in spring training in Orlando, in either 1966 or 1967. I had always wanted to meet the man.

Baseball was the only thing I wanted to do as a young man growing up.

Then I moved to New York and played sandlot baseball. I didn't play high school ball. I played outside Yankee Stadium, I played in Central Park, I played in the Bronx. I remember one day when I was playing outside Yankee Stadium. I looked over at it and I said to myself, "One day, I'm going to be playing in Yankee Stadium."

Major League teams had scouts that went around and saw kids. I was playing shortstop. The Minnesota Twins saw me and liked me and signed me.

When I went and tried out for the team, a guy noticed my arm wasn't strong enough, so he decided to move me to second base.

★ ★ ★ BIG-LEAGUE MEMORIES ★ ★ ★

The one thing that stands out for me was my first All-Star Game in Anaheim in 1967.

I was a young kid, only 21 years old, on the field with Mickey Mantle, Carl Yastrzemski, Ernie Banks, Willie Mays, Henry Aaron, Brooks Robinson, Harmon Killebrew. These were guys that I had grown up admiring, and here I was standing on the same field with all of these superstars. I was nervous. I thought my legs were going to run right out from under my body. It was one of the greatest experiences any kid could have.

When I look back, my memories aren't of the batting titles. It was that day in Anaheim. That was a special day.

Another special day for me happened in late June during the 1977 season when I was hitting .400. I think I received six or seven standing ovations at the old Metropolitan Stadium in Minneapolis.

I went 4 for 5 that day. And every time I got a base hit, or ran on the field, I got a standing ovation. It was something I treasured. It made me feel good.

Obviously it was a thrill getting voted into the Hall of Fame. I remember when I was inducted, on the way to the stage, fellow Hall of Famer Bobby

Doerr came up to me and said, "Rod, welcome to the greatest fraternity in the world." He was right. And now when guys get inducted I always tell them, "Welcome to the greatest fraternity in the world," because it is.

★★★ SUPERSTITIONS ★★★

When I went to spring training I always asked God to give me good health. I'd say, "You give me good health and I'm going to go out and do well and perform for You. I'm not going to ask for this many hits, just good health."

I didn't think I had any superstitions at all. But it's funny. During the 1977 season, I'd always put on my left **sanitary** (sock) first, and then I would always put my left **stirrup** (sock) on. Then I would do the same thing with the right foot. I never put one sanitary on and then the other one.

So one day one of the guys came by and said, "I want you to try something. Try putting on your left sanitary and then your right sanitary."

I said okay. So I put on the left sanitary and I tried putting the other one on, and I couldn't do it. So I put on my left stirrup, like I always did.

I thought that was a habit. I didn't call it a superstition.

MENTAL EDGE

The runner stands on first base, looking at the pitcher on the mound. The situation calls for a stolen base. The runner has the speed to accomplish that task, but he knows that sheer speed isn't necessarily going to make him successful in his mission.

He doesn't know this right-handed pitcher too well. He doesn't know his pickoff move very well.

So when the runner takes his lead from first base, he takes a big lead, knowing that by doing so, the pitcher will throw over to try to pick him off. That will give the runner a chance to see his pickoff move.

The lead is big. The pitcher comes to his set position. And he whirls and throws over to first. The runner, expecting this throw, gets back easily.

But he noticed something. The right-hander's left shoulder is pointed a bit toward first base. That tells the runner that when the pitcher throws to the plate, he has to move that left shoulder toward the plate. And once he does that, he can't throw back to first because that would be a balk.

So the runner takes his lead again. He watches the pitcher intently. The pitcher comes to a set. His left shoulder begins to point toward the plate. Immediately, as it turns, the runner takes off for second.

The close scrutiny pays off. He gets a great jump.

—*S. K.*

GLOSSARY

Bail: To pull away from the plate as the pitch is coming.

Balk: An illegal movement by the pitcher that permits the runners to move up a base.

Bat Head: The fat part of the bat, toward the end.

Bat speed: The velocity of the bat as it travels through the hitting zone.

Deaden: To bunt the ball so it slows and stops quickly as it hits the ground.

Drag: To pull a bunt to the right side as a left-handed hitter.

Drill: To hit a batter with a pitch.

Opposite field: For a right-handed batter it's right field; for a left-handed hitter, it's left field.

Pull: For a right-handed hitter, it's hitting the ball to the left side of the field; for a left-handed hitter, it's hitting the ball to the right side of the field.

Roll over: When one wrist rolls over the other in a swing, generally leading to a weak ground ball.

Sanitary: The long uniform sock, usually white, worn next to the skin.

Secondary lead: As the pitch is delivered, the few extra steps the baserunner takes toward the next base.

Soft-tossing: A hitting drill in which a person kneeling a few feet away and facing the hitter from the side softly tosses a ball over the plate for the batter to hit.

Stirrup: The uniform sock that fits under the arch of the foot and is worn over the sanitary, usually of a contrasting color.

Stride: The step taken as a hitter starts his swing.

Walking lead: When the pitcher is in the stretch position, the baserunner walks off his base, trying to keep his momentum heading toward the next base.

GARY CARTER

Elected: 2003
Position: Catcher
Born: April 8, 1954, at Culver City, California
Height: 6-2; **Weight:** 215
Threw and batted right-handed

A rugged receiver and enthusiastic on-field general, Gary Carter excelled at one of baseball's most demanding positions, as both an offensive and defensive force. A three-time Gold Glove winner, Carter belted 324 home runs in his 19-season Major League career. "Kid," as he was called, was a two-time All-Star Game MVP and an 11-time All-Star. His clutch tenth-inning single in Game Six of the 1986 World Series sparked the New York Mets to a dramatic comeback victory over the Boston Red Sox and, ultimately, a World Series title.

How were you set up in your catching stance?

I was relatively wide with my feet, about shoulder width apart. I wouldn't get much wider because my intention was to get as low as possible so I could give the best possible **target** to the pitcher.

Were you flat-footed behind the plate?

No, not at all. You absolutely have to be on the balls of your feet. I always tried to look at the catching position and my stance as almost being like a linebacker in football. You have to be ready back there for anything: to block a pitch, to block home plate, to get out of the crouch and throw, to go after foul balls.

I was taught early on that if you were on the balls of your feet you could have the quickness you needed. If you were on your heels, you couldn't move as quickly when you needed to in certain situations.

Were both of your feet facing the pitcher's mound?

No. When I was in my crouch I would turn out my right foot a little bit, toward first base, so I would always be in position to throw to second base if a runner was stealing.

When I gave my signals, it was just a straightforward stance. But when I set up to receive the pitch, I always had my right foot out a bit because that helped my quickness.

How did you give a target?

It's very important to give the pitcher a good target.

What I wanted to do was give a target that was low, at the bottom of the strike zone. That's where you want the pitcher to throw the ball mostly. But also, it's easier to move your glove up to catch a high pitch than it is to start with a high target and then have to reach down low if that's where the pitch goes.

Are there any other reasons for giving a low target?

The lower you get, the better the view the umpire has of the pitch. You have to keep in mind that the umpire is looking over your shoulder and that he's the one who's going to call the pitch a strike or a ball. So I would try to stay low and turn the glove so the palm was toward the plate. I would catch the ball out a bit and pull it back into my body.

Is the target always over the middle of the plate?

Your glove may not always be over the middle of the plate, but you always want to keep your glove in what I call the center frame of your body: under your nose and chin, centered on your body.

You want to try and catch the ball in that center frame. If it's an inside pitch, you move your body a little with it, moving over so you can catch it in your center frame. It's the same with the outside pitch.

That's why you have to be on the balls of your feet, so you can move your body more easily into these positions without having to move your feet. You kind of lean a few inches to catch the ball in your center frame.

I almost tried to catch the ball with my mask, because I used to have my glove almost directly in front of my mask.

How was this helpful to the pitcher?

As the pitch came in, if you could move to catch it in your center frame and you gave the umpire a good look at the ball, he might say, "Well, gosh, he caught that pitch right in the middle of his body," and he'd call it a strike.

The pitch might have been a foot inside, but because you caught it in the center frame, it might be called a strike. So, as a smart receiver, the catcher might get more strikes for his pitcher if he catches the pitch in that center frame of his body.

How do you put down signals for the pitcher?

The biggest thing to emphasize is keeping your legs closed as much as possible. And you want to give your signal in the middle part of your crouch, between your legs.

As a right-handed catcher, you put your glove extending past your left shin guard. You keep your right hand in the middle of your legs. You have to be careful of where your hand is when you give your signs because you don't want anybody on the other team to pick them up.

If you get too low, the signals you put down with your fingers might be seen from the other team's dugout. Or the third-base coach or the first-base coach might be able to see your sign.

Why is it bad if the opposition sees your signs?

That would give the batter an advantage.

Some teams like to try to pick up the signs and flash them to the hitter. If I was a hitter and I knew someone who could flash signals to me, I would take advantage of that. It's easier for a batter to hit when he knows what's coming. That's all part of the game.

That's why you want to mix the signals up, especially when there's a runner at second base who can stare directly in to the plate to see the signals. In that case you give a **sequence** of signs, many different signals one after the other. The sequence is something you go over with your pitcher, so you and he both know that, for instance, the "real" signal might be the first one after you put down a "2." There are all kinds of variations along these lines.

Is there a specific sequence of signals you should put down?

You don't want the signs to be too complicated. You want them relatively simple so your players in the field can pick them up, which can help them with their positioning. And you don't want your pitchers to have a difficult time figuring out what pitches you are calling.

What are the basics?

Usually a "1" is the fastball and the "2" is the curveball. But if you always put down "1" first, and then move to the "2" if the pitcher shakes you off and doesn't want to throw a fastball, the batter might figure out your system. He'll know that a curveball is coming if the pitcher shakes off a sign. That would make it easier for him to hit.

How do you receive the ball?

I kept my right hand behind my body so my right (bare) hand wasn't exposed to foul tips.

Did you protect your right hand on every pitch?

I'd do that unless there was a runner on base. Then I would put my right hand, with my thumb tucked, almost like making a fist, right behind my glove.

Why would you do that?

That made it quicker for me to transfer the ball from my glove to my throwing hand in case someone tried to steal a base. This way the transfer was all in one motion: I caught the ball, turned, got the ball in position in my hand, pointed my left shoulder to second base, stayed low, and made a quick snap throw.

If I had my right hand behind my body and then had to bring it around to the glove for the transfer of the ball, that would give the baserunner trying to steal second base some extra steps before I could get rid of the ball.

What is the throwing motion to nail a basestealer?

You don't want your arm going backward past your ear. On this type of throw you're emphasizing more the wrist than the arm.

You snap the throw. That's the quick release you want, and it also gives you more carry on the ball than if you reached back and threw the ball hard the way a pitcher would. That's why they say a catcher has to be

quick behind the plate to throw out a base-stealer, and the quickness comes with the snap throw.

If you're thinking "quick and accurate" rather than trying to throw the ball hard, you'll have more success.

How important are a catcher's feet in throwing out base-stealers?

You throw runners out more with your feet than you do with the strength of your arm.

You need a good foundation and a good setup, which means moving your feet quickly to get your-self in the best possible throwing position. That's why you turn out your foot (right foot for a right-handed catcher, left foot for a left-handed catcher) a little in your stance, to help you get to this body position quicker.

How do you know when a runner's going to try to steal?

You see the runner on first base peripherally. You can see out of the corner of your eye when he starts to take off. You should also be anticipating that he might go, so you won't be surprised and you'll always be ready.

What do you do when you see he's going?

As the pitch is thrown, you don't necessarily wait for it to come to you. You actually start your momentum, getting into your throwing position, as the ball is coming to you.

What you're doing is speeding up your foundation, getting your body turned so you can make the play all in one motion.

How do you block pitches in the dirt?

It's a fine art. The way to accomplish that is to cut down on the distance between a ball in the dirt and you, as the catcher. You go forward to the ball on an angle.

You don't want to move your feet so you just go laterally across the catcher's box area. You actually want to move up a little on the pitch and into the batter's box, where the ball is going to hit the dirt. That helps to minimize the bounce, and it puts you closer to the ball when it hits the dirt, giving you a better chance of blocking the pitch than if you had just moved laterally.

What's the position of your body as you try to block the ball?

Basically you want your body leaning forward at a 45-degree angle. You want to make sure you keep your chin down, and you also want to have the feeling of just softening up your midsection, where the ball will hit.

Why would you try to soften your midsection?

You want to relax everything and let the ball come to you, let it hit you in the chest protector. That softens everything and the ball just falls right down in the home-plate area. That's also why you want your body leaning forward at a 45-degree angle, to help soften the ball and keep it in front of you.

If you tighten up, the ball will have a tendency to bounce way away from you.

I've always said that you should try to catch the ball in the dirt with your chest protector rather than your glove. If you try to catch it with your glove you'll have a tendency to get lazy. You might try to backhand one instead of getting in front of the ball, and the ball can get past you.

★★★ YOUTH BASEBALL MEMORIES ★★★

When I was in Little League growing up in Southern California, I was a big Los Angeles Dodgers fan. So my favorite guys were Sandy Koufax and Don Drysdale. I loved Maury Wills. I also followed Mickey Mantle; I think everyone in my era followed the Mick.

I didn't know much about catching at the time. When I signed I had played mostly as an infielder and as a pitcher. I didn't even really know how to put the gear on when I got to the pros and they told me to catch. I didn't know the clips on the shin guards went on the outside of the legs. I didn't know how to put on a chest protector.

When I was 14, playing Pony League ball, we got to within one game of the World Series. In the last game, there was a kid by the name of Gary Skidmore who I will never forget. I came in to pitch in relief, and I gave up this dribbler kind of hit to Gary Skidmore that got through the right side of the infield and into right field, and it turned out to be the game-winning hit. That is a vivid memory, but a disappointing one.

I played American Legion ball. We played in a ballpark in Fullerton, California, that was shaped like a square. Center field was the furthest spot from home plate. And it had another backstop where kids could play even during a game because it was so far out. In a game during my last year playing American Legion, I hit one over that thing. That is a great memory.

★★★ BIG-LEAGUE MEMORIES ★★★

My favorite memory in the majors has to be winning the World Series in 1986. I was playing for the New York Mets, and we beat the Boston Red Sox. That to me was the epitome of it all. Playing 18 years and having that opportunity to play in a World Series and then being the champions, that was the ultimate.

★★★ SUPERSTITIONS ★★★

If I got hot during a certain time, I would wear the same things. I had my socks kind of marked. If I wore them one way one game and had a good game, I would probably put them on the same way the next game.

I did the same with sweatbands. I had a way of noticing which one was on my left wrist and which one was on my right wrist. And there might have been a favorite undershirt I was wearing. I would wear the same things if I was hot.

I didn't realize it until video became popular in the early '80s, but I used to have all kinds of idiosyncrasies. I would go through the same routine before setting up to hit. I always cleaned the batter's box with my spikes. I hated a dirty box, meaning a lot of footprints. It had to be smooth. I always cleaned off home plate with my hand as the catcher, saving the umpire from having to come around from behind the plate to use his brush. I've always been a little obsessive when it comes to cleanliness, anyway.

MENTAL EDGE

The catcher pulls on his mask, but that doesn't mean he can't see what's going on.

He knows the runner at first is a good base-stealer. So he settles into his crouch and flashes the signals to the pitcher. When the pitcher nods in agreement to the pitch selection, the catcher turns his head slightly, to check out the runner.

How big is his lead? Is he leaning on his front foot? Is he wiggling his fingers, something he only does when he's going to steal?

The catcher has a strong hunch he's going to be running on this pitch. So he gets himself ready, turning out his right foot a little, putting his bare hand right behind the mitt, getting up a little on the balls of his foot as the pitcher begins his motion.

The pitcher delivers the pitch. The catcher sees out of the corner of his eye that he was right. The runner has taken off.

As the pitch arrives, the catcher begins turning his body to get it into the best body position to make a throw. The ball hits his mitt, but only for an instant, the catcher smoothly transferring it from his glove to his bare hand.

He brings his hand up to his right ear as he turns so his left shoulder faces second. And he makes a quick, strong throw to the corner of the second-base bag.

—S. K.

GLOSSARY

Sequence: The order in which signals are given.

Target: Where you want the pitcher to throw the ball. For a pitcher, it's where the catcher holds up his mitt.

✦

ORLANDO CEPEDA

✦

Elected: 1999
Position: First base
Born: September 17, 1937, at Ponce,
Puerto Rico
Height 6-2; Weight 210
Threw and batted right-handed

National Baseball Hall of Fame Library, Cooperstown, NY

A powerful slugger during his 17-year Major League career, Orlando Manuel Cepeda Penne withstood a series of knee injuries to become a seven-time National League All-Star. As a 20-year-old with the San Francisco Giants in 1958, the "Baby Bull" hit .312 with 25 home runs, earning unanimous NL Rookie of the Year honors. In 1967, Cepeda knocked in 111 runs for the World Champion St. Louis Cardinals while becoming the first unanimous NL Most Valuable Player since Carl Hubbell in 1936.

In general, where would you position yourself at first base?

With nobody on, I would play more toward my right, more toward second base, a little wide of first base. How many balls go over the first-base bag? Not a whole lot.

Maybe with a left-handed hitter up I might move closer to the bag, but even so, there are very few balls hit right over the bag. More balls are hit between first and second than down the line.

What about late in a game? Would you guard the line?

You want to play close to the bag in a close game late because you don't want to give up a double. You'll give the hitter a single on a ball between first and second, but not a double where he'd be in scoring position.

What did you do as the pitch was being delivered to the plate?

You have to follow the pitcher's throw to the plate. Your first move is to your right a bit, a little step to get set.

Many first basemen go too far to the right doing this. Sometimes if you move too far, you're going to be off-balance. If you take a short step to your right and you get set, you'll be balanced and able to go either way, to your left or to your right, wherever the ball is hit.

Balance is important, because if you're off-balance, it will be tougher to get to the ball.

What do you do when a ground ball is hit to another infielder?

You want to run quickly to the bag.

Where do you position your feet when you get there?

When I got to the bag on a routine ground ball I liked to put the base between my legs as I faced the infielder. I'd have my feet on the sides of the bag. That way I could go either way, depending on where the ball was thrown.

I would shift my feet. If the ball was thrown to my right, I would move my feet so my left foot was on the bag and I would be able to reach out for the ball.

How would you give a target?

If it was a ground ball to the short-stop, let's say, you want to make sure you give the shortstop a good **target** with your glove. Instead of bending down, you have to stand straight up so he can see you, and you put your glove up at your chest and open it to him because that's where you want the throw, to the chest.

How do you stretch for a low throw?

One thing you have to remember is you don't want to stretch to the ball too quickly. A lot of first basemen do that, even in the big leagues.

You need to see the ball first. If you stretch too quickly, and the ball isn't coming right at you, but is to your right or your left, you won't be able to get it. But you put one foot up against the bag and reach out with your glove.

I used to stretch to get in front of the ball. A lot of times, if it was a **double-play ball,** for instance, and the relay was coming to me, I was careful because I knew the ball can go by you very easily if you stretch.

So sometimes, instead of going out to stretch for the ball, you want to stay back, get in front of the ball and let it hit you and fall in front of you. You won't get the out, but the runner won't get an extra base, which he would if the ball got by you.

What did you do on a ground ball to first?

After catching it, I liked to give the ball to the pitcher before he got to the bag, allowing him plenty of time to catch the ball and then look for the bag.

If you give the pitcher the ball just as he's touching the bag, he has to catch the ball and find the bag at the same time, and that's going to be hard for him.

What kind of throw would you make to the pitcher covering first?

I would throw an underhand toss to the pitcher. Sometimes if it's a close play you have to throw overhand and hard, but most of the time you have plenty of time to make this play, so you underhand the ball to the pitcher, up softly toward his face so he can see it better.

How did you hold on runners?

When I was holding runners, I liked to be in a position to be able to move quickly to my right side, where the throw should go to the bag, so I used to give the pitcher a target so he could see me.

My left foot would be in fair territory very close to the foul line. My right foot would be up against the side of the bag.

What would you do if the pitcher didn't throw over?

When the pitcher threw the ball to the plate, I just tried to make a short stride to my right and turn and face the hitter, ready to go either way with my feet if the ball was hit to me. You want to be balanced as the ball gets to the hitter.

How did you make a play on a ground ball to first with a runner at first?

I tried to make sure I got the out at second base. You have to remember that you have to get the first out before you can the second out for a double play.

That's a tough play for a right-handed first baseman because the runner can be in the way of your throw to second base. But as soon as the ball is coming to you, you have to be ready to turn and throw to second base. You have to get your feet in position and pivot as you're getting the ball.

Where do you go to get into cutoff position?

If there's a runner at second base and there's a base hit to right field, you want to be in the cutoff position between first base and the catcher. If the ball is hit to center field, you go right behind the mound, closer to second base.

You give the same kind of target to the outfielder on his cutoff throw that you give to the shortstop on a ground ball. You get your arms up and your glove out to him so he hits you in the chest with the throw.

What else does a first baseman do if there's a base hit?

If a guy hits a double, for instance, after he rounds first base you follow him to second base. He may not know you're there. The shortstop and the second baseman may be out on the cutoff, so you can sneak in behind him and maybe get him out if he rounds the base too far.

You see, playing first base looks easy, but it's not. You really have to be involved in every play. If you want to be a good first baseman you have to do a lot of things quickly and efficiently.

Can everyone become a power hitter?

You can't teach that. You're born with it. But whether you're a power hitter or a singles hitter, you use the same approach in hitting. Like (Hall of Famer) Ted Williams used to say, you need to have bat control and you don't want to **overswing.**

Every hitter is a contact hitter. You have to make contact. If you make contact and you have power, the ball will go far. If you make contact but don't have enough power, the ball is going to die. So you have to know your limitations as a hitter.

But don't swing too hard. If you have the power, it will fly. If you don't have the power and you hit the ball in the air, you'll be hitting long fly ball after long fly ball to the outfielders, that's all.

How important is it to wait on the ball as a hitter?

I used to try to hit the ball to right field a lot. I used to **go with the pitch** the other way. It's hard to do that. You have to wait so long to go the other way. But I always felt the longer the wait the better. If you wait, you'll see the ball better. You'll see how the breaking ball is breaking.

You need to stay back on the ball. If you can do that, you'll be a .300 hitter. If you try to **pull** every ball, you'll be a .250 hitter. You'll be out in front of the ball too much if you're trying to pull everything. If you stay back, you can wait longer and you can hit the ball to right or left, wherever the ball is pitched.

★★★ YOUTH BASEBALL MEMORIES ★★★

When I was 14 years old I remember I was trying out with a sandlot team in Puerto Rico hoping to play, to have my first uniform. And I remember after the tryout I went to get my uniform, and they gave uniforms to everybody but me. I was very disappointed. I was very sad.

But I didn't give up. I tried out again the next year, and I got the uniform. It was amazing. I slept with it. We used to play on Sundays. I played third base. I was pretty quick. And I hit two home runs the first day.

★★★ BIG-LEAGUE MEMORIES ★★★

Playing in my first big-league game was special, and I have great memories of playing for the St. Louis Cardinals. That was a great ballclub, the best team I ever played on. There were so many great days that it's hard to pick out one or two.

St. Louis was one of the best cities to play in, but when I went to Boston I was very impressed. The fans in Boston were thoroughly committed to the team—the ballpark, everything, was wonderful there.

I went 0 for 11 my first 11 times at-bat for Boston. But my first hit for the Red Sox was a home run against the Yankees. In the bottom of the ninth, I hit a home run off Sparky Lyle. We won the game. The fans liked me then.

★ ★ ★ SUPERSTITIONS ★ ★ ★

I didn't have any superstitions.

MENTAL EDGE

The first baseman has to be like a patient father, understanding his children's different personalities without passing judgment, helping them out when they need the help, making them look good even when they aren't perfect.

On the baseball field, the third baseman, the shortstop, and the second baseman all depend on the first baseman to handle their throws cleanly and get the out at first, especially when the throws aren't chest-high, right to the first baseman's glove. The infielders are all the same in that they field ground balls and throw to first base for the out. But they're all different too. Their throwing styles vary, causing the baseball to act differently as it hurtles toward first base.

The third baseman's throw, for example, may have a tendency to sail. So when a grounder is hit to third, as the first baseman runs to cover the bag, he thinks about that tendency, mentally getting ready to jump for a high throw while figuring out a way to keep his foot on the bag.

The second baseman may have a throw that tails toward the home-plate side of the bag. The first baseman knows this as he covers the bag, so he prepares in his mind to move his feet so he can reach over for the throw and still record the out.

The shortstop's throw may often sink into the dirt a few feet in front of first. So as the first baseman gets to the bag and faces the shortstop, he's getting ready to scoop any ball that might bounce.

And he does all this as calmly as possible. He doesn't shout at an infielder after a bad throw that can't be handled. He doesn't throw up his hands in disgust if a wild throw ends up in the dugout. He knows they're trying their best. Mistakes happen. It's part of the game. But the first baseman has to be mentally and physically prepared for the worst.

—S. K.

GLOSSARY

Double-play ball: A ground ball on which there is the chance to turn a double play.

Go with the pitch: To hit the ball to the opposite field.

Guard the line: To play closer to the first-base line than usual.

Overswing: To swing too hard.

Pull: For a right-handed hitter, it's hitting the ball to the left side of the field; for a left-handed hitter, it's hitting the ball to the right side of the field.

Target: Where you hold your glove to receive a throw from any other fielder.

BOBBY DOERR

Elected: 1986
Position: Second base
Born: April 7, 1918, at Los Angeles, California
Height 5-11; Weight 185
Threw and batted right-handed

National Baseball Hall of Fame Library, Cooperstown, NY

Ted Williams called Bobby Doerr "the silent captain" of the Red Sox. Doerr was a lifetime .288 hitter, driving in 100 runs six times with a high of 120 in 1950. He hit .409 in the 1946 World Series. Doerr once held the American League record by handling 414 consecutive chances without an error.

When the ground ball comes your way, do you want to snatch at it with your glove?

No, you don't want to grab at the ball. If you do that you just won't catch it cleanly. You want to have soft hands, so you can catch the ball smoothly.

How can you develop soft hands?

One thing you can do to help a kid develop soft hands is to take an egg and throw it to him. If you do that, he'll probably grab at the egg and squish it. But after you do it a time or two, he'll be able to catch that egg without breaking it. That's what's called soft hands. And that's what you need to catch a baseball.

How do you position yourself when a ground ball comes to you?

You want to get in position to play the ball in front of you, but you get a little sideways to it so you can scoop the ball and be ready to throw. As the ball comes to you, your hands are well out in front of you. This way you can field anything, even if the ball takes a bad hop, because you'll be able to react to it and bring in your hands to adjust to the ball.

And after fielding the ball, as you bring the glove back to you to get into a throwing motion, your legs will **pivot** to put you in a good position to throw to first.

You want to be balanced on both feet, maybe leaning a shade more on your right side if you're a right-handed thrower.

How do you play a ball hit to your right side, a ball that's up the middle?

You try to play that ball backhanded because if you try to get in front of it, you won't have as much range.

Once you made that play, how did you throw the ball to first?

I would try to catch the ball, plant my right foot, and throw over the top, gripping the ball across the seams because that way I could get a more accurate throw.

Some people on this play could catch the ball going away from first, stop, whirl, jump up, and throw it.

Were you standing still when the ball was pitched?

I was always kind of moving. I didn't walk in toward the hitter when the pitch was delivered, but I had some motion going left and right, so that if a ball was hit, I wasn't at a dead standstill. I had some momentum working for me, so I could get started going to my right or to my left, wherever the ball was hit.

Some people say you should walk toward the hitter as the pitch is delivered, but if you do that and he hits the ball, your first step is going to be forward. And I always felt I wanted to go left or right with that first step because it gave me more range.

How did you make the play if it was hit to your left?

Any time a ball was hit like it was going to be a tough play in the **hole,** my first motion was not going to my left, it was going back and to my left. That gave me a little more range. A lot of times I would make plays on the outfield grass.

How would you throw the ball from there?

On a play like that you have all your momentum going to your left. I would completely pivot all the way around—back toward second base and around to face the first baseman—and then make the throw, pretty much doing it all in one continuous movement. The throw becomes kind of a sidearm throw.

If you tried to stop yourself as you went left to get in a better position to throw, you would lose a certain amount of time with that runner going to first.

How did what the pitcher threw help you position yourself?

At second base I could see the catcher's signals so I knew what type of pitch was coming. Now, if it was a left-handed batter and a right-handed pitcher, and I saw that the next pitch was a curveball, I knew the left-handed hitter was more apt to pull the ball.

So sometimes in those instances I would take an extra half step to my left as I saw the ball going to the hitter because I would anticipate the hitter pulling the ball. And by the time he hit the ball, I had taken maybe a full step. Of course, the ball might get hit up the middle, but that didn't happen too often.

You have to know what pitcher is throwing. It helps.

How do you cover the bag on a steal attempt?

When I got there I always tried to straddle the bag, that is, have the bag between my legs as the ball was arriving.

If you get in front of the bag to take the catcher's throw, the runner can make a slide back behind you and still get to the bag. So sometimes you might miss him. If you straddle the bag, you can protect both sides of the bag, wherever he slides in.

When do you leave your defensive position to go cover the bag?

That's one thing you have to be careful of.

Let's say a right-handed hitter was up, and the pitcher was going to throw a curveball. The batter was likely to pull the ball and hit it toward the shortstop side of the infield, so I would give the shortstop a signal that I would cover the bag.

If I was going to cover I didn't want to move too quickly because that could give something away to the hitter. If he saw me move to cover the bag, then he might know a curveball was coming.

So you try to hold your ground as long as you can without tipping off the opponents to what you're doing.

So when do you break for the bag?

When the runner on first goes, you have to break for the bag. You can't still hold your ground then because you have to beat the runner to the bag to catch the ball. You don't want to be on the run when the catcher is throwing the ball.

How would you know the runner had taken off?

You'd see him taking off out of the corner of your eye.

I hated a guy who would bluff from first base, fake like he was going, because then I'd have a tendency to take a step toward second. And if a ball was hit to my left it might get through because I had already committed myself a step or two toward the bag.

How do you approach catching pop-ups in the outfield?

You go after it thinking it's yours to catch. But any time an outfielder calls you off, you have the understanding that you get out of the way and let him take the pop-up. It's easier for him to make the play coming in than it is for you to make it going out. That was my toughest play.

Did you have any collisions with outfielders while chasing pop-ups?

I broke into the minor leagues with Smead Jolley in right field in Hollywood. He never said anything. You'd go out to get a pop fly and you'd hear this thump, thump, thumping of him running. And if he ran into you he'd knock you head over heels, so you always had a little bit of fear.

But that's a play that should be practiced over and over because you need a good understanding and good communication on those plays between the infielders and the outfielders.

How did you make a play when a left-handed hitter tried to drag bunt for a hit?

You have to make that play barehanded most of the time because you're charging in and it's going to be a do-or-die play anyway. If you try to make that play using your glove to field the ball and then transferring the ball from the glove to make the throw, that's going to give the runner at least one more step on you.

What are the second baseman's responsibilities on a sacrifice bunt?

The second baseman has to go to first base to cover.

Anytime a bunt is in order, you anticipate the bunt being dropped down. You get ready to move to first base because on that play, the first baseman is likely to break in to field the bunt. Even if the ball is bunted to the third baseman, the second baseman has to be at first to get the throw from the third baseman.

★ ★ ★ YOUTH BASEBALL MEMORIES ★ ★ ★

I remember throwing a rubber ball against the steps of my front porch. That was one of the greatest ways to practice. That's how you get soft hands. I did that by the hour.

I played a game with myself. I could throw the ball so it went to my left and I had to go get it, or I could throw it so it went to my right and I had to get it.

We had a playground about three or four blocks from where I lived in Los Angeles. We practiced all the time. I played some American Legion baseball for the Leonard Woods team. We won the state championship in 1932 on Catalina Island, won a regional in Utah and went to Omaha, but we fell one game shy of making the Little World Series.

In the winter some pro players from the minor leagues lived in the area. They'd work out a lot and play ball on Sundays, so we worked out with those guys when I was 13, 14, and 15. I broke into the Pacific Coast League when I was 16, but I played more like an 18-year-old because I had been exposed to professional baseball more than most kids my age.

★★★ BIG-LEAGUE MEMORIES ★★★

I remember opening the 1937 season in Philadelphia. I think I went three-for-five on Opening Day.

I'll never forget going to Yankee Stadium for the first time. What a monstrous ballpark. You felt like a little ant there.

I remember making one play at Chicago one night, about the ninth inning of a doubleheader. Jim Busby was the hitter, and the winning run was on third base. I went over in the hole, and I'll never forget it because it seems like I went an especially long way.

Busby was a right-handed hitter and I caught the ball on the grass, whirled, and got him bang-bang at first base or the game would have been over. That was probably as good a play as I ever made. And we went 18 innings in that game, then went extra innings in the second game too. It was daylight by the time we got back to the hotel.

Playing in a World Series in 1946 was a big thrill. Ted Williams and I used to talk about it. Getting into the Hall of Fame and having your number retired (number 1, by the Boston Red Sox) was great, but winning a World Series would have completed it all. We never did that, though.

I used a small glove so I could get the ball out quicker. It was a Lonny Frey model. I set a record with that glove: 414 chances and 73 games without an error. But I like to look at it another way. Earlier in the season I had a no-error streak going. I had gone 30 games without an error, and then in the next game a pitcher for the White Sox hit me a grounder and it jumped over my glove. It was a bad hop, but in the major leagues they give you an error on that play. After that I went the next 73 games without an error. So I went 104 games with only one error.

★★★ SUPERSTITIONS ★★★

Back when I played we used to leave our gloves on the field between innings, and I always used to leave mine with the palm down. I think sometime when I threw it down like that I might have gone in and hit a home run, so I built up a superstition of having the face of the glove down all the time.

Nellie Fox evidently caught on to what I was doing. One time as I was heading into the dugout, he looked at me and turned the glove so the palm was up. I shook my fist at him.

I think every player has superstitions. I never got into the on-deck circle. I never stepped on the foul lines. And I never let my bats get crossed lying on the ground or anywhere. I still have that superstition. I don't leave anything crossed, not even a fork crossed over a knife.

MENTAL EDGE

Between pitches, the second baseman rarely stands still. He might walk around a bit. He might smooth out the dirt in front of him.

But he's always thinking.

There's a runner at first. He has some speed. Will he try to steal second base on the next pitch? Should I move in a step or two and closer to the bag another step or two so I can cover second base quicker on a stolen-base attempt?

Or will the batter try to drop down a bunt here? Should I move a step closer to first base to allow for that possibility, knowing I have to cover first base on a sacrifice bunt because the first baseman will be charging to field the bunt?

Or will the team try a hit-and-run in this situation, sending the runner to second base on the pitch while the hitter's responsibility is to hit a ground ball through the infield? How quickly should I leave my position to go cover the bag if it's a hit-and-run? I don't want to open a hole in the infield too quickly. That would give the batter a better opportunity to get a hit and move the runner to third.

All these thoughts are racing through the second baseman's mind.

He may look like he's walking aimlessly in circles around the infield dirt between pitches. And he may look like he's auditioning for a job with the grounds crew as he smoothes out the dirt with his spikes.

But he's always thinking, pitch after pitch, always calculating several strategic offensive possibilities and his defensive answers to those moves.

—S. K.

GLOSSARY

Drag bunt: A bunt by a left-handed hitter that is dragged between the pitcher's mound and first base, rolling toward where the second baseman plays.

Hole: For a second baseman, this part of the field is the area between the first and second basemen.

Pivot: To move with your legs and body to get in the best position to make a throw.

★★★★★★★★★★★★★★★★★★★★★★★★★★★★★

DENNIS ECKERSLEY

★★★★★★★★★★★★★★★★★★★★★★★★★★★★★

National Baseball Hall of Fame Library, Cooperstown, NY

Elected: 2004
Position: Pitcher
Born: October 3, 1954, at Oakland, California
Height 6-2; Weight 190
Threw and batted right-handed

Dennis Eckersley blazed a unique path to the Hall of Fame. Over the first half of his 24-year career, "Eck" won 150 games primarily as a starting pitcher, including a no-hitter in 1977. Over his final 12 years he saved nearly 400 games as a closer, leading his hometown Oakland A's to four American League West titles and one World Series championship. He earned Cy Young and Most Valuable Player honors in 1992. Eckersley is the only pitcher with 100 saves and 100 complete games. From 1988 to 1993, Eckersley struck out 458 and walked only 51.

What's the difference between being a starting pitcher and a closer?

One difference is learning how to warm up. That was one of the toughest changes for me when I went from starting to closing, determining how many warm-up pitches I needed.

What happens, though, is because you throw so many warm-up pitches as a starter, you never get confident. You always wonder, "Is that enough?" If you're asking yourself that question, you've thrown too many—you've warmed up too much. You're **blown out** already.

I would play catch, then get on the mound and throw 80–100 pitches, not all of them hard, to get ready for a start.

How did you warm up differently as a closer?

When you get more confidence in doing the closer's thing, you don't need that many pitches to get ready. You remind yourself you don't need many.

The secret is to throw pretty much only to get loose. I mean, how many times can you hit the outside corner on the black with warm-up pitches?

Once you've done it a few times and you're loose, you're ready.

Was your pitching repertoire and approach different in the two roles?

As a starter, you have a pace-yourself attitude. If you pitched every time with the same urgency you need as a closer you wouldn't last long when you went out there. Also, you have to finesse people sometimes because you have to get them out four times as a starter.

As a closer, you want to be aggressive more than anything else. You want to go right at the hitters with your best stuff all the time. I only used two pitches: a fastball and a slider. As a starter I also threw an off-speed breaking ball as a changeup.

What's another major difference between starting and closing?

The adrenaline rush. There's no comparison. And that can be hard to handle.

As a starting pitcher, I completed several games, which means I was pitching in the ninth inning. So I'd been there before. But pitching in the ninth inning as a closer was different.

Even with all my experience, my 12 years as a starting pitcher, I was uptight coming in in the ninth inning. There's so much more pressure on you. If you mess up in the first inning, that's one thing because there's time for your team to come back. But if you mess up in the ninth, you and the team can't come back from it.

How easy is it to manage that adrenaline?

For me, that was the toughest part of the job. That adrenaline was serious, man. It's like a drug. It really is. You don't know how it's going to affect you. It's like taking a sleeping pill. Sometimes you fall right to sleep, sometimes you don't.

When did that adrenaline kick in for you?

There was adrenaline in the morning for me every game day. When the phone rings in the bullpen and you know it's for you, that's when the real shock waves go through you.

How important was it for you to have that adrenaline?

I needed that adrenaline to be the best I could be.

Is there such a thing as a closer's mentality?

I think it's a guy who is aggressive, someone who almost looks angry out there, and a guy who can forget easily. If you blow a save, you have to forget about it and not let it affect the next time you're out there with a save on the line.

Did you have a short memory?

After a bad game I'd want to get into a game again as soon as I could.

People talk about being able to turn the page. But I couldn't turn it until I got somebody out. I couldn't sleep. I lost some tough ones. I had a lot of bad nights, and I had a great career.

The older I got, the failures were even more devastating. But that just should drive you to where you don't want to leave anything unfinished.

It's all about confidence. You have to try to take care of everything you can take care of and realize that there are some things you just can't control.

What was out of your control as the closer?

Once you let the ball go, it's out of your control. They're either going to hit it or they're not going to hit it. Your team is either going to field the ball or it's not going to field the ball. If you've done everything in your power to control what you can control, you should be able to live with that.

How important is it for the closer to look confident, bordering on the cocky side?

I played that look. A lot of times I used it when I wasn't feeling so great, when I wasn't so confident. I'd try to look confident, and I like to think I fooled the hitters sometimes. That helped me get fired up. Sometimes it was more body language than substance, and that worked for me at times.

You have to be aggressive, but you still have to have good control. You have to be able to blow the fastball by guys sometimes, but you have to be able to **paint the corners** too.

How much did you pay attention to the rest of the game when you were a closer, knowing you'd only pitch the final inning?

I'd watch the game and see how it was developing. I didn't miss a trick, seeing what everyone was doing and thinking what I would do when I got out there.

I'd be thinking along with the manager, trying to figure out when he might bring me in, because that helped me get mentally prepared for going into the game.

When you were a starter, what was your opinion of the closers?

Poor things. Most of them couldn't start.

After you were installed in the closing role, how did you look at it differently?

Closing made me feel 20 years old again, because you could be as aggressive as possible for one inning instead of trying to control that aggressiveness and pace yourself.

At the beginning I was just trying to find my way, prove I still had it. I had to accept going to the bullpen or leaving the game. I loved the game. I still wanted to pitch, and closing was my opportunity to stay in the game.

I took pride in being a starting pitcher. I got lucky being a reliever. Both jobs are very important to a team.

★ ★ ★ YOUTH BASEBALL MEMORIES ★ ★ ★

What I recall about being young is that I always wanted to throw a no-hitter. When the first guy got a hit, man, that hurt.

I just remember being dominant as a kid. In my mind I couldn't just be good, I had to be great. I couldn't just get hitters out, I had to really get them out. I didn't want to just **punch out** 7, I wanted 15.

I grew up in the Bay Area of California. There was some pretty good competition. I played Little League, Pony League, and in a couple of Connie Mack leagues with the big boys. When I was 15 I played with the older kids, like 18. That was huge. That was like playing pro ball in the Bay Area, playing with all the best guys, giving you a sniff of what it's like to play at a high level.

I remember playing a Connie Mack game in Santa Clara and facing Steve Bartkowski, who went on to play quarterback for the Atlanta Falcons in the National Football League. My team had just gotten me to pitch. But my first time up at bat I hit a **rocket.** I was only 15. And I hit the top of the fence. I got to second base and I was loving that. I remember that more than pitching. I was just a little kid. They said this guy could really throw, and I hit a rocket off him.

I threw a couple of **no-nos** in high school. I thought I was dominant. I tried to throw as hard as I could.

★ ★ ★ BIG-LEAGUE MEMORIES ★ ★ ★

In my first start as a big leaguer I shut out the Oakland A's, and they were coming off three world championships.

I was 17 and in the California League when I made my first pro start. I was a scared kid who had just left home. But I shut out the Visalia Mets.

I remember winning 20 games when I was with the Red Sox in 1978. That season, in 1978, we had to win every day late in the season to try to win the division. It was really tight. I won my last four starts.

Saving Game 4 of the World Series in 1989 was a better feeling than pitching a no-hitter, which I had done for Cleveland on Memorial Day in 1977. If you had asked me after the no-hitter what might be most special, I would have said the no-no. But I was young. The World Series, that was a team thing, about 162 games in the regular season to get there. It wasn't all about Denny, not like being "Mr. No-No" for a night.

People remember the home run I gave up to the Dodgers' Kirk Gibson that lost Game 1 of the 1988 World Series. Afterward, I don't remember it as being that horrible for me to take. I was in such a good state in my mind back then. I was a recovering alcoholic. I think I was grateful. I think I knew how lucky I was just to be there even though it did hurt.

Two years earlier I had been trying to get my life back in order again, and here I was back on the mound. I knew where I had come from as a person. You're a lot happier when you're grateful. I regret not appreciating playing baseball in the big leagues more when I was younger.

Being a closer suited my personality so well. I remember they used to play the song "Bad to the Bone" when I came into a game. It was like in that "Major League" movie, where they had a character called Wild Thing. That was me, man, that was like magic for me. It really was. I became even better than I was, with the adrenaline kicking in. I had a second chance in life and in baseball, and I wasn't going to waste that.

★★★ SUPERSTITIONS ★★★

I had a lot of superstitions. How you put your socks on: the right one first or the left one. It can come down to that for me. Scary.

I had my favorite undershirt, and I would never touch the foul line. But you would never know I wasn't touching that foul line. I worked my stride so it wouldn't look like it. And the resin bag, get that away from me. I never used it anyway, so if it wasn't where I wanted, I'd kick it over to the other side of the mound. I wouldn't pick it up.

Then it's down to the shoes. Hey, these shoes are hot. But they're getting worn out. I need a new pair of shoes. But how can you change your shoes when things are going so well? And the hat. Dirty hats. I'd change that because I didn't want a stinky hat. I would have several, so one never got too much work. It gets crazy, but I don't think I was neurotic.

There was superstition in my routine to pitch as a closer too. I'd stay in the clubhouse for the early part of the game. I'd stretch my legs, then stretch my arm to get the blood flowing. Then I'd go to the bathroom before I left the clubhouse. Then I was ready.

MENTAL EDGE

Three outs. That's all the closer has to get. What's the big deal?

How can that be different from all the innings in which the starting pitcher has to get three outs? How can that be different from the outs recorded by the other relief pitchers in the game?

Three outs is a piece of cake, right?

But, of course, it's not that easy. When the closer comes into the game, he's being asked to get the final three outs to preserve the team's victory. The game's outcome is in the balance, and the closer holds it in his hands.

His teammates have been sweating and working hard to be able to take the lead and hand it over to the closer. Now they watch. They're hoping, no, make that expecting to see him finish off the opposition for the victory.

No pressure, right? It's just three outs, right?

Wrong.

The closer has no safety net. If he gives up a run and the other team ties the game, he has failed. If he gives up more runs, his team loses without getting a chance to come back. It's over. He blew it.

The stress level is high.

The rewards are great. If the closer gets the three outs without any damage, he's in the center of the field, accepting congratulations from his teammates, basking in the glow of a job well done.

If he doesn't do his job, he's the loneliest player on the field, walking slowly off the mound, shouldering the blame for the loss.

Three outs. What's the big deal? Just ask a closer.

—S. K.

GLOSSARY

Blown out: Tired.

No-Nos: No-hitters.

Paint the corners: Throw pitches over the corners of the plate.

Punch out: To strike out a batter.

Rocket: A hard-hit ball.

BOB FELLER

★★★★★★★★★★★★★★★★★★★★★★★★★★★★★

Elected: 1962
Position: Pitcher
Born: November 3, 1918, at Van Meter, Iowa
Height 6-0; Weight 185
Threw and batted right-handed

Bob Feller's fastball set the standard against which all of his successors have been judged. "Rapid Robert" spent his entire 18-year career in Cleveland, amassing 266 victories and 2,581 strikeouts, leading the American League in strikeouts seven times. Feller, who missed four years while serving his country in World War II, threw no-hitters and 12 one-hitters.

What is "power pitching?"

Power pitching is throwing not only a good fastball, but throwing a fast curve and a hard slider.

How effective is a good fastball?

The best pitch in the world is a good high fastball, one that's in on the wrists, because there are very few good "wrist" hitters who can catch up to that pitch. Guys like Ernie Banks, Barry Bonds, and Yogi Berra had fast wrists, but it's a tough pitch to hit.

If you're a right-handed pitcher and you can throw your fastball up and in to a left-handed hitter, and you can keep your slider in around their belt, where they grip the bat, about wrist high, you can **tie the hitters up.**

Nowadays they use thin handle bats that I call high-swing-speed bats, but you can't get around on those good fastballs no matter how light a bat you use.

How is the fastball different from other pitches?

When you go out there throwing knuckleballs, you're like a dart thrower. And then there are pitches like the split-finger and the breaking balls. Those pitches all tend to break down as they get to the plate.

On the fastball, though, you have backspin on the ball when you release it, so the ball will appear to rise on its way to the plate. Even if it doesn't really rise, it appears to the eye that it is rising, and it looks like it's picking up speed.

Of course, it's not really picking up speed because as soon as you throw the ball it's losing speed because of the atmospheric pressure on the ball. It's like putting your hand out the window of a moving car. You'll feel that wind resistance. There's the same resistance on the ball, but to a hitter it looks like the pitch is getting faster.

What does a power pitcher have to have besides a strong arm?

In power pitching you have to have good legs and stamina.

Generally speaking, the great pitchers who have had great fastballs throughout the history of the game, guys like Roger Clemens and Nolan Ryan and going back even further to Walter Johnson and Lefty Grove, had good legs and stamina.

Why is that important?

You have to use your legs to shove off the pitching rubber to get your body in motion.

That gets all the weight from your right side if you're a right-handed pitcher (or from your left side if you're a left-handed pitcher) into your delivery, which is what you want. You'll get power all the way from your big toe into the end of your fingers from shoving off.

How do you get that push?

You shove off the rubber by bending your knee—pretty deeply—to get the stride you want toward home plate.

How do you deliver the ball to the plate?

You point the toes of your front foot to the exact place where you want your fastball to go, right to the **target.**

Also, I think you should always keep your throwing elbow away from your body. If you bring your elbow too close to your body when you deliver the ball, you're probably going to have elbow or arm problems.

You have to have a strong wrist to throw a fastball.

How does the fastball travel depending on the grip?

A four-seam fastball, which you grip across the seams, maybe with the tips of your fingers resting on the seams, will carry better to the plate. You'll get

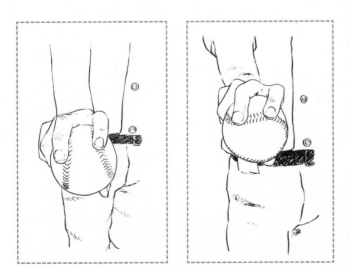

some backspin on the ball, which makes it go more accurately. That ball won't sink.

That's basically the same grip an infielder or an outfielder will use to throw the ball.

If you held the ball with your fingers on top of the seams instead of across them, that would be a sinker depending on how you let it go. But the pitch could also sail if you held it that way. The ball is more difficult to control that way than throwing it with the four seams.

Is there any one way that's best to throw the fastball?

You have to experiment to see which way you want to throw your fastball, or your curve and slider for that matter.

It's a matter of trial and error to see which way you'll have the most speed on the ball, and which way you'll be most comfortable or will have the most control with it. Those things have to be worked out individually. You cannot generalize, because it depends on things like your physical structure, your coordination, and your delivery.

Are there other important components to throwing a fastball?

Follow-through is very important.

When kids are younger they tend to throw with just their upper body, just their arm, and they don't get their legs or their butt into their delivery. But you need to get your entire body into the delivery.

Does everybody follow through the same way?

How you follow through depends on whether you're throwing with a strict overhand motion, or sidearm or three-quarters. Some guys follow through so hard they almost fall down. It varies from pitcher to pitcher.

There's no standardized way to do it. You just let your arm and body continue your delivery nonstop after you release the ball, being as comfortable as you can while getting the most on the ball you can.

It's also a little bit of trial and error to see how you can get yourself in good fielding position after you release the ball.

How do you want to finish up to be in a good fielding position?

After delivering the pitch, you want to keep your glove ahead of your elbow, out a bit toward the hitter.

So if you're a right-handed pitcher, your glove is on your left hand, and after delivering the pitch, you want that glove out in front of you a bit, ahead of your left elbow in case someone hits a **bullet** right back at you. That will help you protect the upper half of your body from a line drive. That ball comes back off the bat a lot harder and a lot quicker than you can throw it up there.

How can a power pitcher maintain his stamina on a hot day?

You have to pace yourself.

If you're facing a hitter who doesn't bother you much, someone who is not a very good hitter, try and make them hit the first or second pitch in the at-bat, especially if there are already one or two outs and you've got a lead late in a ballgame.

You're not worried about that hitter knocking the ball out of the ballpark. You want to get that hitter out of the way and save your good stuff and a lot of your energy for the last few innings, or for the hitters in the lineup who give you the most trouble.

But don't you want to try and strike everybody out?

It's not too smart to be trying to strike everybody out unless you're going for some kind of a record. If you're not going for a major league strikeout record, the best thing you can do is just get the hitter out. It doesn't have to be on a strikeout. That's where pacing yourself comes in because you're trying to win the ballgame.

How do you work on your control?

Whenever you're throwing, even if you're just playing catch, you want to try to hit a target. Whether it's the other guy's belt buckle or right shoulder, find some target and throw at it.

It's always good when you pick up a ball to have an idea where you're going to throw it, so when the time comes that you have to throw the ball accurately—when you're under pressure to hit a target—you're going to do it or come close to it.

★★★ YOUTH BASEBALL MEMORIES ★★★

My memories are mostly from our farm in Iowa, playing with my dad.

I didn't throw balls against barns. That's a myth. I had a rubber ball I used to roll off the roof of the barn, and I'd catch it when it came down. But as a kid, I had no brothers, and my sister was 10 years younger than I, so my dad usually played catch with me. I played on a grade-school team and on a Bible school team when I was on summer vacation.

I was not always a pitcher. I started playing third base, and then short and second. I wasn't much of a hitter. Of course, in high school they're not throwing many curveballs and I could hit the fastball pretty good.

I hit a few home runs in high school, but back then, if you hit a ball past an outfielder, it was probably going to roll until it got to the next cornfield. In Iowa where I was from there weren't fences. But I never got paid for hitting, that's for sure.

I played American Legion ball when I was 13, 14, and 15. I'm the first American Legion graduate in Cooperstown in the Hall of Fame. Ted Williams was number two.

When I was 16, I was playing semipro ball. I averaged over 19 strikeouts a game when I was pitching for the Iowa state champions, a team in Des Moines. In 1934, we played in the first national tournament ever held in America in Dayton, Ohio, and we got beat, 1-0, in the finals. And the next year I was pitching for the Cleveland Indians.

★★★ BIG-LEAGUE MEMORIES ★★★

I think getting 17 strikeouts at the age of 17 stands out from my first year in Cleveland. That happened against Philadelphia in Cleveland.

I also had the first no-hitter ever pitched in Yankee Stadium, in 1946, after I spent four years in the Navy. We won the game 1-0 on a home run by my catcher, Frank Hayes, in the top of the ninth inning. And in the bottom of the ninth inning I had to pitch to the heart of the Yankee batting order—including Joe DiMaggio, Tommy Henrich, and Charlie Keller.

The first man, Snuffy Stirnweiss, got on on an error and Tommy Henrich bunted, sacrificing the tying run to second. Then DiMaggio went 3 and 2, and he grounded out to shortstop, but the runner, Stirnweiss, ended up on third base. But then Charlie Keller grounded out to second on a curveball. Charlie didn't hit my curveball too well, so I wasn't going to give him a fastball.

I had a lot of success. I lost some tough games and won some. There's a lot of luck in the game too. Where the ball goes after the batter hits it involves a lot of luck. Whether it's 10 percent, 20 percent, or 30 percent, who knows, but there's a lot of luck in life, and life is not always fair.

★★★ SUPERSTITIONS ★★★

I am not superstitious at all. I hear about people who have to do things like get a drink of water before they go to the mound, or they won't step on the white line, or they have to wear the same clothing every day. I was not superstitious whatsoever.

MENTAL EDGE

The weather is hot and humid, the kind of weather that can sap a pitcher's strength. The power pitcher knows in the first inning that stamina is going to become a big issue on this day.

He's a strikeout pitcher, a guy who relies on a sizzling fastball and a hard breaking pitch to subdue the opposition. Long counts, with batters fouling off fastballs they can't quite get around on quickly enough to put into play, are not uncommon when he's on the mound.

He likes striking out guys. It's a badge of honor. There's no bigger satisfaction in the batter-pitcher confrontation than to see the hitter swing and miss and slink back to the dugout. See ya.

But it's hot. And it's getting hotter.

The pitcher has a decision to make.

On this day, how important is his personal strikeout total? How important is it that he pace himself a bit so he can maintain his strength and pitch deep into the game?

First-pitch outs count too. Maybe sacrificing a little zip on his fastball and throwing pitches on the corners that the hitters can hit, but can't hit with authority early in the count is the way to go on this hot, humid day.

Maybe then, in the late innings, that strikeout pitch will be there when he needs it. And he'll still be on the mound to throw it.

—S. K.

GLOSSARY

Bullet: A hard line drive.

Follow-through: Completing your arm movement after the ball is thrown, almost as if you were drawing a big circle with your arm.

Target: Where you want to throw the ball. For a pitcher, it's where the catcher holds up his mitt.

Tie the hitters up: Pitch them tight, on the inside part of the plate.

WHITEY FORD

National Baseball Hall of Fame Library, Cooperstown, NY

Elected: 1974
Position: Pitcher
Born: October 21, 1928, New York, New York
Height 5-10; Weight 180
Threw and batted left-handed

The crafty left-hander's lifetime record of 236-106 gave him the best winning percentage (6.90) of any twentieth-century pitcher. He led the American League in victories three times and in earned-run average and shutouts twice. Ford won the 1961 Cy Young Award. He had 10 wins and 94 strikeouts in the World Series, throwing 33 consecutive scoreless innings in World Series action.

Who has the advantage in the lefty-lefty matchup, the left-handed pitcher or the left-handed hitter?

You might pitch differently to every batter, but I always thought I had an advantage because I had a big breaking ball and I could throw it from three different arm angles.

To right-handers I'd throw it over the top or from a three-quarters arm angle. To left-handers I would throw it sidearm or three-quarters.

Why throw the breaking ball to left-handers from those arm angles?

You'd see a lot of left-handed hitters **bail out** against left-handed pitchers.

So what you might do, as a left-handed pitcher, was to throw a sidearm fastball on the outside part of the plate for a strike.

Then you'd come back with a curveball on the outer part of the plate. The hitter would think it was going to be a strike, but by the time they swung, the ball had curved out of the strike zone, not even close to being a strike.

You could get them to **chase** pitches out of the strike zone, especially when there were two strikes. They'd be **guarding the plate,** but they'd still chase because they'd be bailing out, so they couldn't see the pitch as well or guard the outside part of the plate.

Where did you stand on the pitching rubber?

I always pitched with my left foot on the left side of the rubber, facing the batter at the far end. I never changed that. I pitched to everybody from that spot.

I would try to look straight ahead and have my left foot in the corner, and my right foot would be just behind the center of the rubber. I just tried to line myself up to the plate. I felt more comfortable throwing that way to lefties and righties.

What's the best delivery?

You should wind up however you feel most comfortable.

When I wound up I took my two arms and threw them back and then forward, and my glove and bare hand would meet at the top, over my head. But you should do whatever works.

Some guys hold the glove right in front of them with the ball in it, and they throw from there. If they turn their hips and kick their legs the right way it really doesn't make any difference. I just felt comfortable doing it the way I did it in the full windup.

Why did you wind up that way?

I did it more to slow down my motion. Sometimes if you rush your pitches, your arm gets ahead of your legs. If the arm gets ahead of the legs, you won't have good control.

And you'll know immediately when you're not pitching right because you won't feel comfortable. You just have to keep experimenting. After you've been pitching for a while it falls into place.

How much of an advantage does a left-hander have in the stretch in holding and picking off base runners?

All left-handers have an advantage in picking off runners at first.

It's all deception because when the left-hander is in the stretch, he's looking right at the baserunner. It's hard for the baserunner to know if the pitcher is going to go to the plate or throw over to first.

Once in a great while you'll pick a guy off, but the idea is to hold the baserunner as close to first as you can so it's difficult for him to get a jump to steal second, and so he won't automatically go to third on a base hit.

Also, if you hold him close, maybe on a ground ball he won't be able to break up a double play.

How do you hold them close or pick them off?

The whole idea of the pickoff, especially for a left-hander, is to get the runner to think your body is going toward home when really you're going to throw to first base. The deception involves a lot of eye motion and body movement.

You have to be comfortable. Your head could be looking at the first baseman and just as you pick up your right leg and start to kick, you look toward home plate. The runner might think you're going to throw home, but you can still throw to first base.

What can a left-hander do in his pickoff move, according to the rules?

As a left-hander, you have to step not quite toward home plate when you throw to first. You don't have step directly toward first base when you make a throw. The umpire will give you a little leeway.

If your right foot, the one that's going to be up in the air in your delivery, lands somewhere between home plate and first base, at a 45-degree angle, that's all right.

But if a left-hander picks up his right foot and it goes behind his left foot in his delivery, he can't come back and make a pickoff throw to first base. That would be a balk. Once your right foot moves behind your left one, you have to throw to the plate.

So you have to fool around, trying different things for your pickoff move. If you pick your right leg almost straight up, the runner doesn't know at that point whether you're going to throw home or to first, because from that position you can do either.

I would kick my leg up, just as a way to balance my body, and let the runners think I was going home, but at the last second I'd step in the direction of first base and throw.

I didn't have a good move until my fourth year in the big leagues, in 1956. I picked off a lot of baserunners, but then it quieted down because word got around that I had a good move, so the coaches didn't want their runners trying to go on me.

How did you make the pickoff play to second base?

That was what we called a "time" play.

You'd take your stretch, but then there was a signal for a pickoff if you thought that runner was taking an extra step of a lead. When I was coming down with my hand and my glove in the stretch, I would sort of hit myself in the stomach hard. That was the signal. As soon as the second baseman or short-stop saw that, they knew it meant they should break for second and I would whirl around and throw.

What footwork did you use on this pickoff play?

You stay planted on the rubber with your left foot, turn clockwise (spinning toward third base and around) and throw to second. I wouldn't turn the other way and throw to second because that would take too long, and you wouldn't have the momentum you'd want going for you on that play.

Where would you throw the ball?

You want to throw the ball right to the second-base bag. That way whoever is covering doesn't catch the ball on the run and have to reach down to make a tag.

You want to throw it about knee-high if you can. That would be the ideal spot for the shortstop or the second baseman. If you throw it too low, they might have to catch it on a hop, which would make it a very difficult play for them.

How do you throw to second to start a double play?

You lead the guy who is covering the bag.

If he's running to the bag, you throw the ball ahead of him like you're a quarterback in football throwing to a guy going out for a pass. You lead him with a throw maybe 8–10 feet in front of him.

He's running fairly fast over to the base. You want him to catch the ball before he gets to the bag, so he can catch it, step on the bag quickly, and throw to first. Or he can catch it, step on the bag, and jump out of the way of the sliding runner, and then throw to first.

When there was a runner at third base, did you pitch from the stretch or the windup?

If there was a runner at third I wouldn't pitch from the stretch. I don't know why some left-handed pitchers do that. I don't know what they can see. Their back is to the runner. I'd use the windup in those situations.

★★★ YOUTH BASEBALL MEMORIES ★★★

I played first base until I got out of high school. I was a fairly good hitter, but I wouldn't have made it to the big leagues as a hitter.

I was born in Long Island City, and when we were 8–10 years old we used to play games we'd make up. We'd put a square on the side of a building with chalk and throw a tennis ball or one of those pink spaldeens (Spalding High Bounce balls), and everyone in the neighborhood would pitch. Two guys on a side, and we'd play that all day. We played stickball too.

By the time I was 15 or so I could throw a little curveball, but I had no intentions of being a pitcher until I was playing for a **sandlot team.** I played first base for that team. When I graduated from Manhattan Aviation High School in 1946, our sandlot team used to play doubleheaders, and our pitcher got hurt. So I started pitching a game every Sunday, from June to September.

And we won the New York City championship at the Polo Grounds in 1946. It was quite a thing. Our team was 36-0. I happened to pitch at the Polo Grounds, and the game went 11 innings. We won, 1-0.

There were scouts there, and the Yankees ended up signing me.

★ ★ ★ BIG LEAGUE MEMORIES ★ ★ ★

Being in the World Series 12 out of 14 years, that stands out for me.

One thing I enjoyed doing was breaking Babe Ruth's record of consecutive scoreless innings in the World Series even though I didn't know he was a pitcher. I actually didn't know that until the day I broke the record, in 1962.

Different games stand out, like the two shutouts I had in 1960 against Pittsburgh in the World Series.

I remember the time when Jackie Robinson stole home on me in the 1955 World Series, but he was out. Our catcher, Yogi Berra, would swear to it that he was out. The umpire was Bill Summers, who was about 5-foot-5. If you ever see that play again, notice where Summers was standing. He was about six feet behind Yogi, and he had no way of seeing what happened.

He was a good umpire, but on that play he didn't get by the plate to get a good view. He had no idea if Jackie was safe or out. It's the worst I ever saw Yogi react to an umpire.

★ ★ ★ SUPERSTITIONS ★ ★ ★

The only thing I wouldn't do was step on the chalk line. I always made sure I stepped over it. And I never shaved the day before I pitched. That was because when I was younger I would touch the resin bag, and when I brought my hand to my face I would break out.

MENTAL EDGE

The left-hander gets into his stretch position. The runner at first base moves off the bag, taking his lead.

The left-hander is looking right at him. He's almost daring him to get off the bag a little more so he can make a snap throw over and pick him off.

But the runner doesn't even have to take a big lead for that to happen. This is one situation where the left-hander has a big advantage. And he knows it.

This is where a little deception comes into play.

The left-hander makes it very difficult for the runner to get a jump. He looks at the runner. He starts his motion. And he throws to the plate. The next time, he looks at the plate and throws over to first base, trying to pick off the runner, or at least keep him close. The next time the pitcher lifts his right leg up straight and holds it for an instant before deciding to either throw over or deliver a pitch to the plate.

All of which freezes the runner. He has trouble reading the pitcher's motion, making it virtually impossible to get a good enough jump to steal second base.

Left-handers have the right stuff when it comes to holding runners at first.

—*S. K.*

GLOSSARY

Bail out: When a batter pulls away from the plate as the pitch is coming.

Chase: When a hitter goes after a pitch out of the strike zone.

Guarding the plate: When a batter doesn't bail out, making sure the pitcher can't slip a pitch on the outside corner past him.

Sandlot team: A team made up of neighborhood kids who didn't belong to a specific sanctioned league.

HARMON KILLEBREW

Elected: 1984
Position: Third base, first base, outfielder
Born: June 29, 1936, in Payette, Idaho
Height 6-0; Weight 210
Threw and batted right-handed

In his 22-year career with Washington, Minnesota, and Kansas City, "Killer" slugged 573 home runs. He tied or led the American League in homers six times. Killebrew hit at least 40 homers in eight different seasons, and knocked in at least 100 runs in nine seasons. He was the American League's Most Valuable Player in 1969 when he led the league in home runs, RBIs, walks, and on-base percentage.

Is there a secret to hitting for power?

Hitting for power is much like throwing the ball hard or running fast.

You have to have a certain amount of ability, and you can improve on that. But by and large, if you're not blessed with some physical ability, you're never going to be a power hitter. You have to realize and understand what kind of hitter you are and get the most out of your particular ability.

How important was pulling the ball in hitting the ball out of the park?

When I was 18 years old, I was hitting for a high average, hitting the ball all over the park.

I talked with (Hall of Famer) Ralph Kiner in spring training, and he saw I had some power. He told me in order to hit a lot of home runs, I'd have to **pull the ball** more. He suggested I move up on the plate and pull the ball.

So I tried that and sure enough it worked. My average dropped, but I felt in the long run I was more helpful to the ballclub by pulling the ball and hitting more home runs.

How did moving closer to the plate help you pull the ball?

It helped because balls that were on the outside part of the plate now looked like they were more right down the middle of the plate, and you could get the bat on the ball and pull that pitch.

What about the inside pitch? Didn't that jam you?

I developed a stance and a stride so that if the ball was on the inside part of the plate I could still hit it and keep it fair. Obviously I got **jammed** like everybody else, but I could still keep balls fair instead of hooking them foul.

That's something I developed over time by trying different things. When I first came up I was a wild swinger with a big swing. Over time I developed a short, quicker swing. I became a more patient hitter, and I learned the strike zone better, so I was more selective. That comes with experience, knowing pitchers and knowing yourself.

Where does the power come from?

Your power comes from everywhere: your arms, your legs, and your hips.

I think your hips start your swing, and then you have to have quick hands, which means from your elbows down to your hands. You need that quickness in your forearms to be quick about a foot through the hitting zone. **Bat speed** is so important.

How did you strengthen your forearms?

When I was a kid, they told us we shouldn't lift weights because it would make you muscle-bound and your swing wouldn't be fluid. We know now that's certainly not true. If you lift weights in the proper way it's going to be helpful.

So if you didn't lift weights, what did you do?

I talked to (Hall of Famer) Ted Williams a lot about hitting. He gave me some good tips on strengthening my arms.

He used to do things like tie a rope to the middle of a broomstick and tie weights to the other end of the rope. Then he would hold out the broomstick at arms' length, parallel to the floor and roll the weights up slowly and then roll them back down slowly, keeping the arms out from the body about chest high. That really built up the forearms and wrists.

So I did that, and I also swung a heavy, weighted bat in the wintertime. That helped with bat speed because when I switched from the heavy bat to my regular bat, it felt much lighter.

Did you swing for the fences all the time?

I played the game according to what the score was and what the situation was in the ballgame. A lot of people thought I was swinging for a home run every time I was at the plate, but that was certainly not true.

Were there times when you did try to hit a home run?

I hit a lot of home runs when I was trying to, but I struck out, popped up, and hit a lot of weak ground balls when I was trying to hit home runs too.

I've heard guys say they never hit a home run when they were trying to, and I know that's not true for me. There were situations in a game that called for the long ball. So in those situations I tried to do that.

How helpful is it to be ahead in the count in those situations?

That certainly helps. If the count is 3-and-0, 3-and-1, or 2-and-0, you're up there looking for a pitch in a certain spot. And if you know the pitcher, you have a pretty good idea what he's going to throw.

So if you're ahead in the count, you want to look for a type of pitch in a certain spot. Up until two strikes you might look for the type of pitch you like to hit best in an area where you like to hit it best.

What was your favorite pitch and area?

Everybody likes to have a medium speed fastball right down the middle of the plate. But for some reason, no pitcher wanted to throw the ball there.

You made the shift from third base to first base. What was the biggest difference?

The biggest problem I had moving from third to first in the beginning was the change of gloves. The first baseman's glove was a lot larger and longer.

At third base, you catch the ball in the middle of the glove most of the time, unless you happen to get a line drive that sticks in the web. At first base, you try to catch the ball in the web all the time.

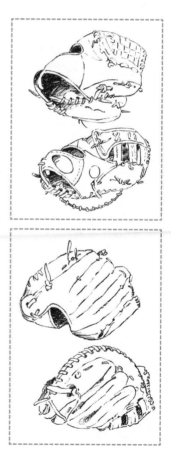

As a first baseman, what's the first thing you have to do when a ground ball is hit to another infielder?

You want to get to the bag as quickly as you can so you can give the fielder a good target.

Once you get to the bag, where do you put your feet?

I would get in a position where I had my heels touching the inside edge of the bag, on the side of the bag that was facing second base. Then if I had to, I would stretch out to catch the throw.

What do you do as the ball is being thrown to you?

When the throw is coming you want to move toward the ball. And you want to watch it all the way into your glove. That's basic. There are very few first basemen who can catch the ball without looking at it. Go meet the ball.

How did you stretch out to catch a low throw?

I would keep one foot up against the bag and stretch with the other foot.

Which foot would you keep on the bag?

You see a lot of guys stretching with the wrong foot.

As a right-handed first baseman it's a lot easier to put your right foot up against the bag and stretch with your left leg. I always felt you could stretch a lot further that way.

How do you handle **short-hop throws?**

You have to have soft hands for those throws that hit the dirt just in front of you. You put your glove out, but then you kind of "give" with those throws, bringing the glove back into you as the ball skips. And you want to soften your hands a little so the ball sticks in the glove.

The toughest kinds of throws to handle are the ones that sail or sink. If the ball takes off, it's tough to grab it.

★★★ YOUTH BASEBALL MEMORIES ★★★

Believe it or not—and it's hard for people to believe this now and even when I was playing—but I was one of the fastest runners on my team when I was a kid.

My father was a track man, and he taught me a lot about running. I once got a medal for the fastest speed running the bases when I was 14. In a football uniform I was the fastest one on the field.

But even then I wasn't a singles hitter. I still had some power as a kid.

The one game I'll always remember was the last game I played in semipro baseball after I graduated from high school.

I had talked to scouts from every ballclub but one. I had not intended to sign at that time. I planned to go to college. They weren't giving baseball scholarships much in college, so I had accepted a scholarship to play football and baseball at the University of Oregon. I was a high school All-America quarterback.

Anyway, we were playing semipro ball. U.S. Senator Herman Welker, from my hometown of Payette, Idaho, became friends with Clark Griffith, owner of the Washington Senators.

The Senators weren't winning many games back then, and Senator Welker kept telling Mr. Griffith about this kid in Idaho he thought could help the Senators. I think, more than anything else, just to keep Senator Welker quiet, Mr. Griffith sent his farm director, Ossie Bluege, out to Idaho.

I'm sure he had no intentions of signing me. He just came out and told me the Washington Senators would like me to go to Washington to work out with the team. I told him I appreciated the invitation, but that I was going to go to the University of Oregon.

It rained that day, and it didn't look like we were going to play. If we hadn't played that game, Mr. Bluege would have probably gone back to

Washington and that would have been the end of that. I would have gone to the University of Oregon. But we did play that night.

Now, I had been going to that park since I was a little kid. And I had never seen anyone hit one over the left-field fence in that park. It was over 400 feet down the left-field line. Well, that night I hit one over the left-field fence.

The next day Mr. Bluege went out, found the ball in a beet field past the fence, and said it was 435 feet. He thought that was a pretty good hit for a 17-year-old, so he called Mr. Griffith and said they should try to sign this kid. So Mr. Griffith gave him the okay to leave a contract in Senator Welker's law office.

It turned out to be a bonus contract. In those days—the early fifties—there was a rule that if you signed for anything over the minimum salary, you had to stay in the big leagues for two years. It's laughable now, but $6,000 a year was the minimum salary. I signed a three-year contract for $6,000 a year plus a $4,000-a-year bonus.

★ ★ ★ BIG-LEAGUE MEMORIES ★ ★ ★

My first home run in the big leagues was against the Detroit Tigers.

I was 18 years old, and there was a veteran left-hander by the name of Billy Hoeft pitching. When I came to the plate, their catcher, Frank House, said, "Kid, we're going to throw you a fastball."

I was young and naïve, and I didn't know whether to believe him. I didn't know if they were really going to throw me a fastball or not.

But sure enough, here came the fastball and I hit it out of the ballpark, probably the longest home run I ever hit in Griffith Stadium in Washington.

As I came around the bases and touched home plate, Frank House said, "Kid, that's the last time we're ever going to tell you what's coming."

★★★ SUPERSTITIONS ★★★

One thing I tried to stay away from was superstitions. I've always felt that baseball is tough enough to play normally without some kind of superstitious rituals you have to do every day: wearing the same clothes, or touching certain things.

I talked to Hank Greenberg one time about superstitions. "Hank," I said, "did you ever have any superstitions?" And he said, "Just one." "What was that?" I asked. And he said, "Every time I hit a ball out of the ballpark I like to touch each base." And I said, "That's the kind of superstition I like."

MENTAL EDGE

A key spot has arisen in the game. The bases are loaded.

As the hitter steps into the batter's box, he knows what pitch he wants to hit. He's looking for a fastball, preferably on the inner part of the plate. That's the pitch he likes to pull and hit for power.

The pitcher knows the hitter. He doesn't want to give him a fastball. He knows the hitter can crush the fastball. So he tries a breaking pitch on the outer part of the plate.

The hitter recognizes the spin on the ball. It's not a fastball. He doesn't swing. The pitch breaks out of the strike zone for Ball One.

The hitter is sticking with his game plan. He's looking fastball all the way. The pitcher sticks with his game plan, not wanting to give in and throw a fastball. He tries another curve.

Again, the hitter recognizes the spin. He doesn't swing. This pitch also sails out of the strike zone. The count is now 2-and-0.

The hitter knows he's in a good spot. The pitcher knows he's in trouble.

The pitcher can't afford to walk this hitter. A walk will force in a run. He has already missed with two breaking balls. What should he throw next?

The hitter knows that the pitcher can't afford to miss with another breaking ball and fall behind in the count at 3-and-0. It's easier to throw a fastball for a strike.

So the hitter looks again for the fastball.

And here it comes. The hitter, his patience rewarded, takes his best swing at the pitch he knows he can drive.

—*S. K.*

GLOSSARY

Bat speed: The velocity of the bat through the hitting zone.

Jam: A hitter is jammed when a pitch on the inside part of the plate leaves him unable to get the good part of the bat on the ball.

Pull the ball: For a right-handed hitter, it's hitting the ball to the left side of the field; for a left-handed hitter, it's hitting the ball to the right side of the field.

Short-hop throw: A throw that bounces close to the fielder. It is just enough out of reach so that he can't catch the ball with his glove before it hits the ground.

BILL MAZEROSKI

Elected: 2001
Position: Second base
Born: September 5, 1936, at Wheeling, West Virginia
Height 5-11-1/2; Weight 183
Threw and batted right-handed

In 1954, 17-year-old Bill Mazeroski signed with the Pittsburgh Pirates as a shortstop, but he was moved to second base. There he became one of the best defensive players at the position with a lifetime .983 fielding percentage. The 10-time National League All-Star led the league in assists nine times, in fielding percentage three times, and in double plays eight times. Mazeroski, who had 2,016 hits in his career, achieved hero status in Pittsburgh in 1960 when he became the first player to end a World Series with a home run, leading the Pirates to the title over the New York Yankees.

When a double play was in order, how would you position yourself differently for a right-handed hitter before the pitch was delivered?

It all depends on the hitter. Usually it's just about where I would play the particular hitter normally, but then I'd cheat a little bit, maybe walk in a couple of steps. Everybody has to cheat a little bit so you can get to the bag a little quicker.

Where would you play for a left-handed hitter?

If it was a left-handed home-run hitter, you'd play him to **pull** mostly, over toward the **hole,** because very rarely would he hit the ball to the shortstop.

But you still have to play close enough to the second-base bag to be able to turn the two. You can't play him way over in the hole because if he does hit the ball to the shortstop, you have to be able to get to the bag.

How does the pitcher influence where you might play in a double-play situation?

The type of pitcher has a big effect on where you play. It depends on how hard he's throwing, how often he throws off-speed stuff, and how he's trying to pitch a guy, which in the big leagues is all discussed before the game starts.

If you talk to the pitcher before the game, you'll know how he wants to pitch to the hitter. That helps you know where to play him, because where the pitch is going to be tells you where he most likely will hit the ball.

Did you look to see the catcher's signal to help you determine where you'd play a hitter?

Some guys like to see the catcher's signal and know what's coming and some guys don't. I never did because I didn't want it to influence the way I played. If I knew the curveball was coming to the left-handed hitter, for example, I'd find myself leaning toward the hole, thinking he'd be pulling the ball.

And if he pushed it up the middle, I didn't get as good a jump because I was expecting him to pull the ball. I thought I got a better jump on the ball not knowing than by anticipating.

With a right-handed hitter up, how would you get to the bag on a grounder to the left side?

I liked to get to the bag before the ball got there from the third baseman or the shortstop. I liked to get there and get my left foot on the bag, so I didn't have to be running and looking for the bag at the same time.

I'd run hard, and I'd run straight at the guy who was getting the ball, whether it was the third baseman or the shortstop. That was so I could make sure I didn't give him a side **target,** where he had to lead me or anything. He could throw the ball straight at me. That made it easier on him, and the throws were much better.

The main thing was, I wanted to find the bag quickly and get that part of the double play out of the way.

What was your rhythm in being the **pivotman** *on the double play?*

When I'd see the ball coming, I did it differently from most people. For most second basemen there would be a 1-2-3 way of making the double play—catch the ball, step, and throw.

But for me, instead of doing it in that 1-2-3 rhythm, I would go 2-1-3: step, catch the ball, and throw. I felt I was quicker that way.

To catch the ball, take the step, and then throw takes more time. If I got the step out of the way before the ball got there, I just had to catch the ball and throw it.

Timing is crucial on a double play. Everything is a lot quicker. And anything to be faster helps you out. To me, everything has to be very short and quick. If you catch the ball and take a big step to get out of the way of the runner, it seems to take about a half-hour to get the ball over to first.

How concerned were you about the runner sliding in to **break up the double play?**

You can't be worried about the runner. You have to make the double play. That's what you're thinking. The runner is always forgotten until after you've made your throw.

How would you make your pivot?

That depended on the throw I got. If the throw was right to me, and I already had my left foot on the bag and my right foot toward left field, I would catch the ball and throw it to first.

If I got a good throw, the bag would protect me most of the time from the runner. I just stood there and let him come. He had to slide over the bag to get me because I'd be throwing from behind the bag, on the outfield side of it.

How would you turn the double play if you didn't get a good throw?

If the throw takes you out of position, then you adjust and go where the throw takes you. Catch the ball and throw to first as accurately and as quickly as you can.

The cardinal sin is anticipating a good throw. You have to be ready for the throw to be anywhere so you can adjust to it and still turn the double play. If it's a good throw, right over the base and at the chest, anyone can turn that one.

How much of an advantage was it to come across the bag in turning a double play?

I never did come over the bag because it takes too long to set your feet when you try to do it that way. Once you get over the bag, you have to set your feet to make a throw to first, and when you do that, you're taking a bigger step.

The quickest way I found to turn a double play was to stay right there, take the step before you catch the ball, and then throw it.

I see guys come across the bag all the time. They're trying more to get out of the way of the runner than to make the double play. It takes too much time to take that step toward third base as you come across. It takes extra time to get that foot down if you take a long step, and you're not going to get as many guys at first base that way.

What are the most important parts of your body in turning two?

Quick hands, quick feet. Your hands and feet work in unison.

If your feet are fast, your hands are going to be fast. I'd move my feet before I caught the ball and get that part of the play out of the way so I didn't have to take time to move them later. It's all in one motion. And it's quick.

What did you do with your hands?

I used two hands. I used my glove hand kind of like a basketball backboard. I'd have it on top, with the fingers pointing up, the palm facing the shortstop or the third baseman. And I'd have my right hand below it, palm up, the wrists close together.

The ball would hit right in the middle of the glove, right in the pocket, and rather than close the glove and catch the ball, I would just bank the ball off my glove to my right hand, just push the ball down to my bare hand.

Catching the ball and transferring it to my throwing hand in one continuous movement gave me my arm speed.

Why did you use this method?

Any time you catch the ball in the glove and then go get it with the throwing hand, that takes extra time. And you don't have time to spare on double plays.

It's different from what most people do. It's not hard to do, but it takes a little practice. It works. It's almost foolproof. I don't know how many I turned, but I didn't drop very many.

How do you start the double play after fielding a ground ball up the middle?

You catch the ball and give the shortstop a little underhand throw as he's coming across the bag. That's about it.

When you do this, you always get your glove out of the way so he can see the ball. Just drop the ball off for him with an open palm toss. That's easy

enough to do because you're moving that way anyway when you're fielding the ball up the middle.

This isn't a regular throw. It's just a little lob, and he moves into it as he moves across the bag to turn the double play.

How do you start a double play on a ball to your left, toward the hole?

If you're going to your left and you can get in front of the ball, you might catch the ball, drop your right knee onto the ground, turn, and throw. Or going this way you might just pivot and throw.

When you make this throw, it's more from a three-quarters arm angle. But again, you get your glove out of the way so the shortstop can see the ball all the way.

What if you can't get in front of that ball in the hole?

Any time you have to reach for the ball going to your left, you turn around toward the outfield because you're moving that way anyway. Then you plant your right foot and you throw to second.

How hard a throw do you make to second?

That throw is a short-arm, accurate throw. You don't want to overpower anybody. You want to give the shortstop a ball he can handle and then quickly get out of his glove to throw to first for the double play. You don't want to throw the ball too hard or you'll **handcuff** him. You want to make a nice, firm throw, usually right at his chest because that's where most shortstops like it.

How can you improve communication between the shortstop and the second baseman on this play, which requires such teamwork?

I always thought shortstops and second basemen should switch positions, taking turns playing each other's position during practice.

Gene Alley and I would do that in spring training. That way I could see what he wanted from me, and I could show him what I wanted from him in terms of where we'd want the throw and when we liked to get it.

You never want to handcuff your partner, so we learned how to make it easy for each other.

What are soft hands, and how are they important to an infielder?

To me, soft hands are two hands working together. If I'm catching a ground ball I want both hands working together. And if I want to get the ball out of there quick, I used my backboard system of catching the ground ball.

How did you field a basic ground ball?

What I did was a little different. It wasn't the "alligator thing" that so many kids are taught, with the glove on the ground, palm up, and the throwing hand

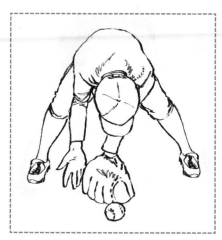 

over the glove, palm down, ready to come down like the top of an alligator's mouth, closing after the ball goes into the glove.

When I caught a ground ball, the little finger of my right hand was under the little finger of the glove. That's how I learned to catch as a kid, using tennis balls. I always used two hands to catch them because they could bounce out of my grasp easily if I only used one hand.

So I'd have my two hands together. When a ball would come, I'd reach out with my hands, and then pull them in as the ball was getting into the glove. That makes the hands soft.

You don't catch the ball in the pocket of the glove, you catch it out near the little finger with your other little finger underneath. You just hold your hands together, and the ball already is in your hand, ready to be thrown. You don't have to reach for it again. You never have to give it that **double clutch.**

How is this method beneficial?

It makes it easy to get rid of the ball quickly after you catch it.

Your right hand becomes an extension of your glove. With the little finger of the right hand underneath the little finger on the glove hand, it creates one big glove instead of two separate things, the glove and the bare hand.

If you put down one hand for a ball hit hard to you and it hits the little finger of the glove, the ball will spin off. If you put two hands down with the little fingers overlapping, you'll catch that ball.

What size glove did you use?

I used a small glove, but not an ultra small glove. I just didn't use the web on it very much. When you want to be quick, you can't use a big glove. You just want to use the part where it stings the most—right in the middle of the hand—because you can get the ball out of there quickly to make a throw.

★★★ YOUTH BASEBALL MEMORIES ★★★

All I ever did was throw balls off the wall. Tennis balls, rubber balls. That's how my hands got quick. I'd use two hands because if you tried to catch the ball with one hand without a glove it was tough.

And I didn't have a glove for a long time when I was growing up. To get my first glove I had to dig an outhouse hole. It was a two-seater. My uncle told me if I dug that outdoor toilet hole, he'd give me a glove. So I dug it, and I got my first glove. I was 10 or 11 at the time.

Before that I had always borrowed someone else's. In those days we always played **pickup games.** When the kids on the field came in to bat, they'd throw their gloves down at their positions, so I could use theirs.

I played on a team in our little town, Rush Run, Ohio, and we played other little towns. We had bake sales and things like that to buy our uniforms. We probably played 30 to 40 games a summer, which was a lot. I was just barely in high school at that time. I was one of the younger kids.

★★★ BIG-LEAGUE MEMORIES ★★★

Of course, there was the home run I hit in the bottom of the ninth in Game 7 that won the World Series in 1960.

I thought we had the game won before that, though. We were up two runs going into the ninth after Hal Smith's home run in the eighth. All we had to do was get three outs in the top of the ninth and we would be the World Champs.

But the Yankees came back and scored two runs and tied the game in the ninth. After their half of the inning I was sitting on the bench, all depressed. I had forgotten I was in the on-deck circle when the eighth ended.

Then someone said, "Hey, Maz, you're up."

So I walked up to the plate, thinking about how I could just get a base hit—hit the ball hard somewhere, get on base, get this thing started.

The first pitch came and it was a little high, up around my chin. I can remember the catcher, Johnny Blanchard, walking out in front of the plate, hollering, "Get the ball down."

So the pitcher got it down. And I hit it up.

I hit it hard. I knew when I hit it, with (Hall of Famer) Yogi Berra playing left field, that he wasn't going to catch the ball. I knew it was over his head, but I didn't know if it was out.

So I took off running as fast as I could. After I rounded first and I was going to second I looked down and saw the umpire giving the home-run signal. The fans were going crazy, so I figured it must have gone out. From the time I hit second base I don't think I touched the ground all the way around to home plate.

An opportunity like that doesn't present itself very often.

The most home runs I hit in one year was 19. I think I hit 16 in 1960. Forbes Field was a big park, 365 feet down the line and 430 feet to left-center.

I felt like I could turn a double play about as well as anybody in the world. That's one thing I could do. I'd rather turn a double play to win a game than hit a home run to win a game—except maybe for that homer in the 1960 World Series.

★ ★ ★ SUPERSTITIONS ★ ★ ★

I didn't have superstitions. Not really, not a lot anyway. Maybe not stepping on the foul lines, but nothing else really stands out. Everybody has some little thing they do, but I guess I was sort of boring.

MENTAL EDGE

It hasn't been the best of games for the second baseman.

At the plate, he's 0 for 4. He has struck out twice, popped up to the catcher, and bounced out to the pitcher. He hasn't had a good swing all night.

And in the field, he bobbled a ground ball for an error early in the game, helping the other team score two unearned runs.

But it's the last inning now. Despite his rough game, the second baseman's team is ahead by a run.

The other team is threatening to at least tie the score. There are runners at first and third with one out.

The second baseman forgets what he has done earlier in the game. He has to. Only one thing matters now: If he can turn a double play, his team will win. All he needs is for the pitcher to get the batter to hit a ground ball to the left side.

He notes that there's a right-handed hitter at the plate. It's likely he'll hit the ball to the left side. So the second baseman moves in a couple of steps and moves over to the bag a step or two.

The batter hits a sharp grounder to the shortstop. The second baseman quickly gets to the bag. He takes the throw from the shortstop, deftly moves the ball into his bare hand, and fires a quick strike to the first baseman.

Double play. Game over. His team wins. The second baseman went an ugly 0 for 4 and committed an error. But the double-play ending is as sweet as it gets for the second baseman.

—*S. K.*

GLOSSARY

Break up the double play: To slide into the fielder turning the double play, knocking him down so he can't make the relay throw to first.

Double clutch: To have to reach into the glove twice to grab the ball because the first attempt wasn't successful.

Handcuff: To make a hard throw that is in close to the receiving player's body, making it difficult for him to catch.

Hole: For a second baseman, this part of the field is the area between the first and second basemen.

Pickup games: Neighborhood games in which kids often choose up sides to pick teams. Not necessarily games in an organized league.

Pivotman: The player turning the double play.

Pull: For a right-handed hitter, it's hitting the ball to the left side of the field; for a left-handed hitter, it's hitting the ball to the right side of the field.

Target: Where you want to throw the ball.

PAUL MOLITOR

Elected: 2004
Position: Designated hitter, infielder, out-fielder
Born: August 22, 1956, at St. Paul, Minnesota
Height 6-0; Weight 185
Threw and batted right-handed

As a member of the Brewers, Twins, and Blue Jays, Paul Molitor was a seven-time All-Star who batted over .300 in 12 seasons, stole over 500 bases, and compiled a 39-game hitting streak in 1987. Molitor had a record five hits for Milwaukee in Game 1 of the 1982 World Series. In 1993, Molitor was named World Series Most Valuable Player in Toronto's championship. He retired with 3,319 hits.

Where should you be in the batter's box when you're bunting for a sacrifice?

Whatever approach you take to get into your bunting position, whether it's a **pivot** or an actual movement of your feet, you try and do it in a fashion that gets you a little closer to the plate as well as moving a little bit up in the box.

Why do you want to be closer to the plate?

That can help prevent you from **jabbing** at pitches on the outer part of the plate. It also gives you better plate coverage.

When you move up in the box, it improves your chances of having a better angle with your bunt down the lines, toward third base or toward first base.

The farther back you are, the less margin for error you have. When you're up in the box, that ball you hook a little will stay fair. If you're back in the box, it will go foul.

What is the position of the bat for a sacrifice bunt?

In the squared position, you try to start with the bat parallel to the top of the strike zone. That's the main thing.

That way, any pitch you bunt that would be a strike will be either at or below your bat level. You always want to go down with the bat, because if you're moving your bat up to bunt the ball, that

increases your chances of popping the bunt up instead of putting it on the ground, which is what you want to do.

What problems can arise in moving the bat down to bunt the ball?

When you go down to bunt a pitch, it's important to remember to keep the bat parallel to the ground. If you dip the **bat head** more toward the ground, it will

cause sidespin on the ball when you hit it, which can cause inaccuracy on the bunt you're trying to make.

What do you do with your body to increase your chances of making a good bunt?

You want to bunt with a little flex in your knees. And you want your hands to be relaxed.

It's kind of like catching the ball with your bat. You "give" with your bat a little bit as the ball makes contact because you're trying to **deaden** the ball in one direction or another, either along the first-base line or the third-base line.

How do you bunt for a hit as a right-handed hitter?

There are a couple of different methods. One thing you want to do, though, is try to hold off on showing the bunt as long as possible. But, that being said, you have to find the timing that works for you, because if you start to bunt too late, it puts you in a bad position to make a good bunt.

You have to aim for that fine line between not showing the bunt too soon and getting into position too late.

What's the first thing the batter can do?

Some people do a drop step with the back foot, moving the right foot back behind to put themselves in a better running position once the ball is bunted.

Where should the bat be?

As a right-handed hitter, the main thing is to make sure you have the bat out in front of the left side of your body. And you also want to make sure you keep your bat in that parallel position as you adjust to the pitch.

If you leave the bat below your hip, then the bat head is almost right below your face. And that's a problem for two reasons. First, it's harder to **track** the ball to the bat that way. Second, it's dangerous because the foul balls can injure you, coming up and hitting you because of the bat angle. So keep the bat out in front, off your left hip.

How do you deaden the ball when bunting for a base hit down the third-base line?

Some people try to bunt the ball toward the end of the bat instead of on the **sweet spot.** Hitting the ball on the last 3 or 4 inches of the bat deadens the velocity of the ball coming off the bat and increases your chances of killing the ball in the grass. That takes a lot of practice. It's a tough thing to master, but it certainly helps when you have a guy throwing hard and you don't want to bunt the ball too hard to the third baseman.

How do you bunt the ball to the right side for a hit?

That's a push bunt. Again, you want to keep your hands and bat parallel to the ground at the top of the strike zone. And when you push that bunt between first and second, you want to use a consistent push with both the left and right hands.

When you try to throw the bat head toward the ball, usually the right hand becomes more dominant and you have a tendency to lose the direction of the bunt. Then you wind up getting the ball too close to the pitcher, allowing him to make the play.

How do you bunt as a left-handed hitter?

The sacrifice bunt is the same from both sides. But in bunting for base hits, there are two methods I see left-handed hitters use.

One is where you drop your back foot almost pointing to the back of the plate, but keeping your foot in the batter's box. As you do that, your head crouches down closer to the plate so you can get a good look at the baseball, holding the bat parallel at the top of the strike zone. You do this without crossing your feet. You keep your head behind the baseball, trying to bunt the ball down the third-base line.

Other people will use a crossover method from the left side. As the pitch is coming, they will cross their left foot over their right foot, still keeping the bat head back with an angle to deaden the ball toward the third-base line.

This method helps you get out of the batter's box a little more quickly, but it's hard to do without moving your head. And when you're moving your head, the ball looks jumpy, which makes it tougher to be as accurate a bunter as you would like.

How hard do you want to bunt the ball?

When you're pulling the bunt to the right side of the infield, whichever method you use with your feet, you have to make sure you bunt the ball firmly.

You want to try and entice the first baseman to leave his position to field the ball, which gives you an opportunity to beat the pitcher to the bag for a base hit.

On a sacrifice, where should you try to bunt the ball?

The general rule with a runner on first is to try to bunt the ball toward first because the first baseman can't leave his position until the pitcher has delivered the ball. That decreases his chances of getting the force-out at second base.

With runners at first and second, teams use different defenses to prevent the sacrifice bunt from being successful. The general rule in that situation, though, is to bunt the ball firmly to third base to make the third baseman field the ball. That allows the runner from second to get to third base easily.

What defensive plays might the opposition use?

As the level of baseball goes higher, as defenses get better, there are wheel plays.

Usually the shortstop will cover second base on a bunt, and the third baseman might hang back, with the pitcher trying to cover the bunt down the third-base line.

But on the wheel play, the third baseman charges and the shortstop covers third base. The first baseman charges, too, so the bunter has to try to deaden the ball as best he can in any direction. Another option is to pull back on the bunt, fake it, and try to whack the ball past everybody.

What variables help you decide where to bunt the ball?

Maybe you have a poor defensive fielder on one side of the field. Or maybe the pitcher doesn't move very well. You might try to take advantage of such situations.

If you have a left-handed first baseman, and there are runners at first and second, you want to bunt the ball to third because a bunt to first is an easier play for a left-handed first baseman to make than for a right-handed first baseman.

Knowing where to bunt is just a matter of having a feel or an instinct, once a pitch is delivered, of who's charging and where you can drop the ball to have the best chance of advancing the runners. That strategy should be predetermined.

Peripherally, if you can see them crashing from both first and third, then go ahead and pull the bat back and try and hit it past those guys: the old butcher-boy play, they call it.

When are the best situations for dropping down a bunt for a hit?

Leading off an inning is a very good time to bunt for a base hit. Getting on base to begin an inning is the best way to start a big inning.

If you are someone who can steal a base and get yourself into scoring position after a successful bunt, then bunting might possibly be a worthwhile venture with one or two outs and nobody on base.

When should you not consider bunting for a base hit?

With two outs I don't like the play as much unless you know you can get to second base on the first or second pitch after getting on base. Otherwise, I'd like to see you swing the bat with two outs. Maybe you can hit a double to get yourself in scoring position.

If you bunt for a hit, it's still going to take two hits to score you, and the odds of that happening with two outs aren't as good as they are with one out or no outs.

Are there any exceptions?

To me, the exception with two outs is if you're trailing by multiple runs late in the game and you need baserunners to try to get back in the ballgame. The "rules" for me change a little bit then.

If, for instance, there are runners at first and second and two outs, and you're trailing by four runs, and you see it's a situation where you can bunt for a base hit and the guy on deck can hit the ball out of the ballpark, all of a sudden a little bunt and one swing of the bat and you've got a tie game. If the bunt possibility is there, go for it in this situation.

I also liked bunting for base hits if the leadoff man in the inning had gotten a base hit, maybe early in the game. The pitcher is a variable here too. Does he throw a lot of sinkers? Are your chances of hitting the ball on the ground greater than hitting a ball in the air or a line drive, which would mean you might hit into a double play?

Maybe you've got some speed. Maybe your ace is pitching that day, and you figure if you can get him a couple of runs early in the game that might be enough to win. If so, you might try to bunt for a base hit right there, knowing if you're successful you'll have first and second with no one out.

Even if you get thrown out on your bunt, you'll have a runner in scoring position at second base, and you've got guys behind you who might give you a chance to get a lead or get a run on the board.

Are there any drawbacks to trying to bunt for a base hit with a runner at first?

There are a few reasons I don't like bunting in this situation with one out or no outs. If you try to bunt to the right side and you bunt the ball too firmly, a good first baseman, especially if he's left-handed, can still get the force-out at second.

If you make a bunt back to the pitcher, he can get the force at second. And if the second baseman is playing at double-play depth, it's easier for him to make a play on a bunt to the right side than if he were playing back when you normally would try to bunt the ball to that side of the field with nobody out.

How about bunting with a runner at third base?

There are times when no one in the ballpark is expecting a bunt. You get a guy on third base with two outs, and you don't even have to be a great bunter to be successful. If you drop the ball down firmly toward third base you're going to get a hit and the run is going to score. That's definitely a good time to look to bunt.

Another situation where it might be a good idea to try to bunt would be with runners at first and third and one out with a double-play-type pitcher on the mound, a pitcher who gets a lot of ground balls. In this situation you want to be sure you can get the run in. So you try to push the ball to the right side and deaden it a bit. You might not get a hit, but you'll get the run in and stay out of the double play.

Any other situations where a bunt might be helpful?

Well, if there's a man on second with nobody out, and you're a right-handed hitter facing a sinkerball pitcher, you know it's going to be really hard to hit the ball to the right side to get the runner over to third. So instead of trying to hit a pitch over there, I'd tell you to put a bunt down the third-base line. You might get thrown out, but you'd do your job and get the runner over to third with one out.

When does baseball etiquette dictate that you shouldn't bunt?

There are some unwritten rules on when not to bunt for a hit. It's a little gray in terms of score and inning, though. Is a five-run lead too big for you to be bunting? The other team might take offense. And in what inning do we try to stop doing those things? If my team is losing by 5–0, 6–0, 7–0 in the middle innings, I might still feel we could win the game. So if they're giving me a bunt opportunity, I might **drop one down** to get a rally started.

How did your batting stroke change?

My swing became more compact. I made adjustments as I went along.

I had a pretty average-length **stride** when I started, with more movement in my bat load. I cocked my hands back and changed the angle of my bat before I'd swing. Then as I played and found out I had trouble staying back on breaking pitches, and I would **chase** pitches with two strikes, I needed to find a way to see the ball a little longer. So I would practice with almost no stride. I'd try to use my hands to put the ball in play with two strikes and take advantage of having some speed.

It turned out over time that I got so comfortable with this approach that I incorporated it into my regular swing, where I had minimal stride, if any, at times. I just picked the weight up off the ball of my front (left) foot and set it back down without my foot physically coming off the ground.

How did having a minimal stride help?

It kept my weight transfer from getting out on my front foot too quickly, which I would do if I was striding. I could keep my weight on my backside until I recognized the pitch, and then follow with a nice weight transfer at the proper time instead of going too early.

At the same time this approach helped me keep my head still so I could see pitches a little bit longer, deeper into the hitting zone, before I had to make a commitment to the ball. As everyone learns in math, the shortest distance between two points is a straight line, and this way I felt I was able to get my hands and the bat head to the ball as quickly as possible.

You want to be able to repeat what you do to get in a ready position. The more often you can repeat everything in rhythm, the more successful you're going to be.

So when you have minimal movement, not a lot of things can go wrong. You have fewer problems with weight transfer, the hands moving too much, putting your front foot down in enough time, having your head bobbing and weaving, or getting out front.

How important is rhythm in becoming a successful hitter?

To me, being a good hitter has a lot to do with having everything in sync—aligning your front side to the pitcher and having your hip and shoulder in the proper position—when you swing. Everything has to work together. If the hip turns too soon, if the shoulder flies open, if the hands drop, that's when things break down.

The more those things stay in a synchronized rhythm, the better chance you'll have a consistent swing. By minimizing the movement you have prior to the actual swing, you can increase the percentages of your swing being repeated consistently.

Are there any drawbacks to having a short stride or none at all?

I think you sacrifice power. Some hitters generate power with a leg kick. Guys with bigger leg kicks and longer strides tend to create better leverage. Guys with a little more torque with the bat, that is, guys who keep their hands cocked a little farther away from the pitcher, are able to create more power because of the arc of the swing.

It's like a golf swing. If you just take your club up to your shoulder and swing, you won't hit the ball as far as the guy who gets good hip turn and good shoulder rotation and gets the club pointed out to the target line. That arc generates more club speed and therefore more distance.

How important is bat speed for a hitter?

Bat speed is an important factor in increasing distance. It creates the velocity of the ball coming off the bat at contact. The more crisply the ball comes off the bat, the better chance you have to get the ball through the infield or out of the park.

It's funny, but it's not always the strongest guy who has the best bat speed. A lot of it is being gifted in how you use your hands and get the bat through the hitting zone.

What size bat should you use?

I used a 34-inch, 32-ounce model. But I think you should just experiment as you go through your high school and college years. You're still growing. You want to find something that's comfortable for you.

For me, being a line-drive hitter, I wanted a bat with a bigger sweet spot as opposed to a bat that had a lot of weight at the top. I had a more balanced bat, with an elongated sweet spot.

What does "keeping your hands inside the ball" mean, and how can it help a hitter?

If you keep your hands closer to your body on the path of your swing, your hands are "inside the ball" longer as you swing. It's almost like pushing the ball out there when you hit it, like on an inside-out swing.

I guess it's easier to explain the contrast, which is "casting out." That's where the first thing you do is throw the bat out and around the baseball, creating more of a hook swing, kind of like casting a fishing line.

Keeping your hands inside the baseball gives you a better chance to adjust to the ball, when you see whether it's a breaking ball or fastball. This also prevents you from getting jammed and lets you spray the ball around the field a little better.

★★★ YOUTH BASEBALL MEMORIES ★★★

Playing on a lot of good teams with good players and having good coaches helped me climb the ladder in professional baseball more quickly.

When I was playing for Cretin High School, we won the Minnesota state championship. I was a pitcher as well as a shortstop.

In my junior year, my spot to pitch came up in the championship game. I pitched a one-hitter, and we won in a shutout. That was memorable.

My senior year I played shortstop in the championship game. We were playing a school called Fridley Grace. It was a pretty close game, and I got up with the bases loaded. I got to a 3-0 count.

Now, I was pretty good about looking for signs, but the coach had let me hit 3-0 all year. So for whatever reason, I didn't take much of a look down at the coach to see the signals. I guess he gave me a **take sign,** but I didn't see it. I swung and hit a grand slam.

Normally our coach, Bill Peterson, wasn't too forgiving about guys missing signs, but he let that one slide. After the grand slam, as I was running out to my position on the field, the coach stopped me and said, "You know you had the take sign." But he kind of smiled, so I knew he wasn't too mad.

★ ★ ★ BIG-LEAGUE MEMORIES ★ ★ ★

Most of the memories are team memories. But from a personal standpoint, the first big-league game is special for every player.

I was shipped out to the minor leagues a week before Opening Day in 1978, but (Hall of Famer) Robin Yount got injured, so I was called back to Major League camp. Instead of going to Triple A, I was going to be in the big leagues on Opening Day, playing in front of a sellout crowd in Milwaukee only a half-year out of college.

I had tremendous butterflies that day. I only had a few days to get used to the fact that I'd be the Opening Day shortstop for the Milwaukee Brewers. That was a little overwhelming. As a kid I'd had dreams and aspirations of being in the Major Leagues, emulating players like Harmon Killebrew in my backyard, and all of a sudden I found myself on a Major League infield playing a game.

We were playing the Baltimore Orioles. Their pitcher was Mike Flanagan. I remember grounding out in my first at-bat and hitting a line drive up the middle in my second at-bat for my first hit.

My first Major League game was special, but to have it on Opening Day was even more special.

There were other personal memories, such as my hitting streak in 1987. I'll never forget the drama and excitement of being able to extend it to 39 games. The reaction of the crowds was phenomenal in Milwaukee near the end of the streak. I had played 10 years at that point, so I was able to differentiate between the pressure of a personal run like that, and trying to hold onto a two-game lead with five games to play during a regular season pennant race. I tried to have fun with it, knowing eventually it would end. I wanted to ride it out as long as I could.

In the game that broke the streak, I was facing John Farrell, a rookie pitcher I hadn't had any experience with. I went 0 for 4. I struck out and grounded out three times.

In the last inning I was on deck with two outs and a man on second base, and the score was tied. Rick Manning got a base hit and knocked in the winning run, so I didn't get a chance for another at-bat. As a hitter in the on-deck circle, you always have to let the runner know what to do. I went to the plate and put my hands up to tell him that there was no play, that he didn't have to slide. But I always joke that really I was telling him to go back to third so I could bat again and have another chance to keep the streak going.

Another special moment came in 1992 when I was playing for Toronto and we were in the World Series. Joe Carter hit a home run to win the Series. I was lucky enough to be on first base when he hit it. We had two guys on and were down by a run.

When Joe got a hit to left field, I thought the ball might hit the wall and that if I scored from first we'd be World Champions. But the ball cleared the wall, and finally, after 16 years in the big leagues, I was in the winner's circle. The more you play, the more you realize that you find the most enjoyment in the game when you have a chance to be a World Champion.

★ ★ ★ SUPERSTITIONS ★ ★ ★

My biggest superstition was to try not to be superstitious.

But in saying that, I also know I was a very routine-oriented person. I did the same thing in the on-deck circle every time, I did the same thing at the plate every time. I'd dig a foot hole, step out, take one practice swing, check the signs, get back in the box, and get ready to hit.

I wasn't concerned about what route I took to the ballpark. I didn't wear the same T-shirt every day. I tried not to depend on too many things like that.

MENTAL EDGE

The runner at third takes a few steps off the bag. There are two outs, and the game is tied in the bottom of the final inning. The right-handed hitter steps in to face a pitcher he hasn't much success against in his career.

The pitcher's fastball can be overpowering. It's his best pitch. And his breaking balls aren't too shabby, either. The hitter knows his odds of coming through and knocking in the winning run aren't too good.

But he also knows he's able to handle the bat. And when he takes a quick peek down the third-base line, he sees that the third baseman is playing back.

The hitter has an idea. The element of surprise, he thinks, might work in his favor. There's a lot of grass between home plate and where the third baseman is playing.

He knows the pitcher will start him off with his best pitch, a fastball. And he makes up his mind what he wants to do with it.

The fastball sizzles in to the plate.

The hitter pivots his body a bit, holding out his bat in a good bunting position. The ball meets the bat. The ball rolls about 40 feet down the third-base line on the grass.

The third baseman has no chance to make a play on it. The pitcher has no chance to make a play on it. The runner romps home with the winning run as the hitter crosses first base with a bunt single.

Who says a winning hit has to be a smash deep into the out-field gap?

—S. K.

GLOSSARY

Bat head: The fat part of the bat, toward the end away from the hands.

Bat speed: The velocity of the bat as it travels through the hitting zone.

Chase: To go after a pitch out of the strike zone.

Deaden: To bunt the ball so it slows and stops quickly on the ground.

Drop one down: To lay down a bunt.

Jab: To poke at the ball instead of smoothly moving the bat to the ball.

Pivot: To turn or twist the body to get in a good bunting position.

Stride: The step(s) taken as a hitter starts to swing.

Sweet spot: That part on the barrel of the bat, between the label and the end, where the bat is most solid, contributing to hitting the ball as well as possible.

Take sign: A signal from the third-base coach that tells the batter not to swing at the next pitch.

Track: To watch closely.

PHIL NIEKRO

Elected: 1997
Position: Pitcher
Born: April 1, 1939, at Blaine, Ohio
Height 6-1; Weight 180
Threw and batted right-handed

During his 24-year career, Phil Niekro did not rely on velocity but on a fluttering knuckleball to frustrate big-league hitters. He compiled a lifetime record of 318-274. Twice "Knucksie" led the National League in wins, propelling Atlanta to the National League West Division title in 1969 when he recorded 23 victories, 21 complete games, and a 2.56 earned-run average. Niekro, a five-time All-Star, tossed a no-hitter against San Diego on August 5, 1973.

Is the knuckleball thrown with the knuckles?

A lot of people think a knuckleball is thrown with the knuckles on the ball, but it's really not.

How do you hold a knuckleball?

There are different ways to throw it, but I held it basically like most guys do.

I would get the ball back in the hand, deep in the palm, and I would wrap my pinkie finger and thumb around the ball. Then I would dig the fingernails of my index finger and my middle finger into the ball so I could get a firm grip on the ball. That's how I learned to throw it when I was a kid.

How carefully did you take care of those two fingernails?

That was my life, those two fingernails.

I did very little off the field during my career when it came to those two fingers. I was afraid to do woodwork. I was afraid to do anything that might affect those two fingers. I'd hire people to do things I could have done, because I was afraid if I injured one of those two fingers, my career was over.

How did you take care of them to throw the knuckleball best?

I filed my fingernails so they could give me the best grip. I bit them. For some reason, I have very strong fingernails. Good and hard. I made sure I kept them the exact length I wanted them so I could grip the knuckleball the way it was most comfortable for me.

Where do you dig into the ball?

I would dig my fingernails just off the seams of the baseball.

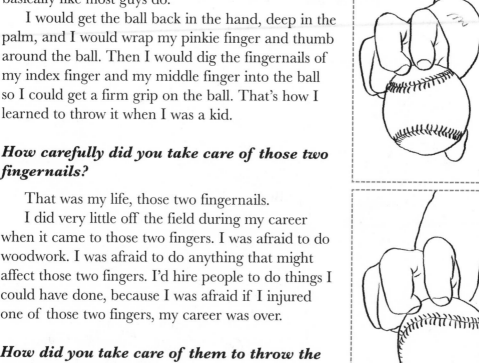

Why not dig them into the seams?

You don't want to do that because if the ball comes out of your hand and one of those seams nicks the fingernail, that's going to start the baseball rotating. You don't want a knuckleball to have any rotation at all.

What do you want the knuckleball to do once it leaves your hand?

The object is not to let the ball turn, or rotate, once it comes out of your hand. A knuckleball is not coming to the plate at a high rate of speed. If a batter sees which way the ball is rotating, he'll know which way it will break and that will make it easier to hit.

A knuckleball pitcher wants the ball coming to the batter with no rotation so he has to figure out which way the ball is going to go. Even the pitcher doesn't know all the time. That's why you see so many batters swing at so many knuckleballs out of the strike zone. They have to wait until the last second to determine which way the ball is going, and by that time, it may be out of the strike zone.

How do you throw a knuckleball?

It's pretty much a stiff-wristed pitch. Your elbow, and your arm all the way up to the top of your shoulder, stays pretty stiff when you deliver the ball to the plate. You kind of push the ball to the plate. You can't allow any turn of the wrist when you let go of the ball because if you do, the ball will start rotating. You do not want any rotation on a knuckleball. I've never been able to throw a good curveball because you need looseness in your wrist to throw that pitch, and my wrist was stiff all the time.

In that way, throwing a knuckleball is different from throwing any other pitch.

What's the best arm angle to use when throwing a knuckleball?

I've thrown it overhand, three-quarters, and from the side. It's basically the same pitch, but you can throw it from different angles and at different speeds. The batter is seeing the same pitch, but he sees it coming out of my hand and away from my body from three, four, or five different areas.

Why is that important?

The knuckleball pitcher is in a unique situation. Even before the ball is thrown, the batter knows what pitch is coming. The pitcher could actually tell a batter, "Okay, here comes a knuckleball," and then let it go.

When a batter goes up there, he knows exactly what pitch is coming, every time, pitch after pitch. So he has a tendency to hit the mistakes, those knuckleballs that don't **dive** or **float** away, because he knows what the pitcher's speed is and where his **release point** is.

I wanted to make the batters think a little more at the plate: "Well, I know he's going to throw a knuckleball, but how hard is he going to throw it? What arm position will he use?" I didn't want him thinking that it would be a knuckleball down the middle of the plate. I wanted him thinking about a lot of things even though it's the same pitch every time. That way I had a chance to mess up his timing and make him less comfortable at the plate.

How difficult is it to control a knuckleball?

It's difficult. But I think you define "control" a little differently for a knuckleball pitcher than for a pitcher who throws fastballs or breaking balls.

Most pitchers can say, "Okay, a fastball up and in" or "a slider down and on the outside corner," and put the ball where they say it's going to go.

But when you're throwing a knuckleball you can't do that. Basically you just throw it down the middle. If you can throw a knuckleball over the plate 7 out of 10 times, or maybe 4 out of 5, then you've controlled it. You want to throw it on the plate where it's swing-able. If you can get that ball someplace in the strike zone where the batter has to swing at it, you have a better chance of getting him out. That's control for a knuckleball pitcher.

You mean you can't hit specific spots in the strike zone with the knuckleball?

I don't know of one knuckleball pitcher who can say, "Knuckleball on the outside corner" or "knuckleball high and in," and then put it where he says it's going. That's because the knuckleball is the only pitch I know of that never does the same thing twice because it's moving without rotation.

I think a lot of guys thought I knew where I was throwing the ball, and I tried to make guys believe I knew exactly where it was going. And sometimes, depending on the wind conditions and the exact place from which I released the ball, I had a pretty good idea of where it was going. But as far as pinpointing that pitch, I don't think anybody can do that.

How much of a role do weather conditions play in throwing and controlling a knuckleball?

The wind plays a big role. When I warmed up for a game, I had to figure out where the wind was blowing from, and that would tell me what adjustments I would have to make.

I'd have to figure out where I had to start the knuckleball out of my hand and how hard I could throw it. It would take me quite a few warm-up pitches before I could figure out how the weather we had that particular night would affect what the knuckleball would do at certain speeds and from certain release points.

What are the toughest weather conditions for throwing a knuckleball?

I always felt that in the cold weather the ball seemed to be more glossy, more slippery, and that made it more difficult to control.

If the wind is in your face, the knuckleball is harder to control, but it will break a lot more. If the wind is behind you, there's no force against the knuckleball as it goes to the plate. The wind then will have a tendency to kind of push the ball to the batter, without the opportunity to break that much.

What are the best wind conditions?

It's best to throw into a light wind. I always liked wind that was blowing from third base to first base. That would keep the ball down more.

It looks so easy to throw a knuckleball, like there's very little physical effort. How tired do you get after throwing a knuckleball?

When a game is over I will be as physically and mentally tired as anybody going out there and throwing 90 miles an hour.

But I didn't need a lot of strength in my body, as far as my legs and back are concerned. There is less movement in the delivery, fewer twists and turns, so I didn't have a tendency to get as tight as other types of pitchers. I never iced my arm down after a ballgame.

I'd throw as much as I could. I got tired arms, heavy arms, just like other pitchers, but I didn't force my arm as much as a guy who threw harder.

Still, mentally it's a tough pitch to throw because it's tough to control. And physically it's a tough pitch to throw too.

A knuckleball is tough to catch too. How difficult is it to handle mentally when even a good knuckler, a strike, dances away from the catcher for a passed ball?

That really wasn't my problem. I got paid for throwing it. If that organization wanted me to pitch, they had to find someone to catch it.

I couldn't change my pitching because the catcher couldn't catch the knuckleball. But I got sent down from the big leagues one time because of that. I got called in and was told they were going to send me to Triple A because no one could catch my knuckleball.

I just said to myself that my knuckleball is good enough to use in the big leagues, so if they want me up here, they'll find someone to catch me. And they did.

How different is it throwing the knuckleball from the stretch position?

There's no difference.

After fielding a ground ball, did you automatically throw knuckle-balls to first or second base?

That never happened. I knew I couldn't throw a knuckleball to one of the fielders because it would be hard for them to handle. When I reached into my glove I grabbed the ball and threw it the same way an infielder would.

I played a lot of infield in high school, and when I was in the pros I worked a lot on fielding ground balls.

★★★ YOUTH BASEBALL MEMORIES ★★★

I remember playing catch in the backyard with my dad, who taught me the knuckleball.

We'd choose up sides in my little hometown of Lansing, Ohio, picking guys and girls to fill up our teams. And that was the pitch I could throw that would get hitters out.

In high school I had the **roundhouse curveball,** and I threw fastballs, but not well enough to open anybody's eyes as far as scouts were concerned.

After I graduated from high school, I pitched for a coal-mining team in Blaine, Ohio, where I was born. It was the same team my father had played for when he was a coal miner.

One day I wasn't pitching, and we were playing the best team in our league. It was top of the ninth, we were winning by one run, and the other team loaded the bases. Our manager called me in. I threw nine pitches and struck out the side. They were nine knuckleballs.

A scout happened to be sitting up there. I think he took notice of me. When I went to a tryout camp later, that same scout was there. "I've seen this guy," he said, "and I know what he can do." That's how I got signed, because I threw a knuckleball.

★★★ BIG-LEAGUE MEMORIES ★★★

One spring I was with the Braves and Brooks Robinson was with the Orioles. We trained in West Palm Beach, Florida, and the Orioles trained in Miami. One night they came to West Palm Beach for an exhibition game. And our lights were really, really bad.

At the time, Brooks Robinson was the guy in baseball. He was an elite player. He came up to face me, and I threw him a couple of knuckleballs. I missed the strike zone, so then I decided to throw a fastball, to see if I could get a strike in there. But the ball got away from me. It was inside and high.

Brooks was probably looking for a knuckleball. I surprised him more than anything. When you throw so many knuckleballs and then throw a fastball at 75 miles an hour, it can surprise someone. And the lights weren't good. He turned, and the pitch hit him on the side of the helmet. His helmet cracked.

He dropped to the ground. They came out and carried him off. When I got back into the dugout after the inning they said they took him to the hospital for X rays. I said to myself, "Why did it have to be Brooks Robinson, of all people?"

I really thought I was going to get a call from the commissioner that night saying, "You just hit Brooks Robinson. We can't have you in this league. We can't hit guys like that in our league." I thought I was going to get released. I thought there would be a lot of stuff coming down on me.

That didn't happen, though. You never want to hit a guy, but that scared me more than anything.

I remember a lot of things about my big-league career. I remember my second game, against the old Houston Colts. I remember my 100th, 200th, and 300th wins. There was a no-hitter and a couple of championships we won.

But one memory that stands out is when I wasn't even playing. A scout came to my house and sat in my parents' kitchen. I was sitting with my mother and my father, my sister and my brother, and the scout offered me a $500 bonus to sign with the Milwaukee Braves minor league system. I jumped all over that offer. I took it. I got $275 a month to play in Eau Claire, Wisconsin.

To this day I realize how fortunate I was to get that opportunity, to get that break, to put my name down on a minor league contract and work for a big league organization in its minor league system.

Another favorite memory was when I was pitching for Cleveland. We were playing a home game, only about three hours from my hometown Lansing, and I beat Detroit. That win gave me and my brother Joe a total of 530 big-league wins. We passed Gaylord and Jim Perry for most wins by brothers in the big leagues. They had 529. That win was great for Niekro family pride, for Lansing pride, for Ohio pride.

★ ★ ★ SUPERSTITIONS ★ ★ ★

I didn't have any. I just went to bed when I wanted to. If the grass needed cutting I cut the grass, even if I was pitching that day. It didn't matter to me.

MENTAL EDGE

The knuckleball is dancing.

It has been darting and diving and floating like the unpredictable path of a butterfly. That's just the way the pitcher wants it. The hitters have been flailing away at the maddening pitch all game without much success.

But there's one problem. The knuckler is dancing so well that the catcher is having a difficult time catching it, even though he is using the larger catcher's mitt that is allowed to handle the pitch.

Indeed, that's how the baserunner got on in the first place. He swung and missed a good knuckleball for strike three, but when the ball got past the catcher, he ran safely to first base.

Another pitch got away from the catcher, so he took second. And when yet another pitch sailed off the mitt and rolled to the backstop, he made it to third base, only 90 feet away from tying the score.

The knuckleball pitcher takes a deep breath. The poor catcher is doing his best, but it just isn't an easy pitch to catch. Now, with the runner at third base, should he keep throwing the knuckleball, knowing that one more passed ball or wild pitch will result in a tie game?

It's an easy question for the knuckleball pitcher to answer. Here it comes, another knuckler. It's his best pitch. If it gets away from the catcher, it gets away. So be it. There's no use throwing a lesser-quality pitch just because you're afraid one might get away.

That's life for the knuckleball pitcher.

—*S. K.*

GLOSSARY

Dive: To sink.

Float: To sail.

Release point: The position of the arm and hand when the ball is thrown to the plate.

Roundhouse curveball: A big-breaking curveball, one with a big arc to it.

BROOKS ROBINSON

Elected: 1983
Position: Third base
Born: May 18, 1937, at Little Rock, Arkansas
Height 6-1; Weight 190
Threw and batted right-handed

Known as the "Human Vacuum Cleaner," Robinson played 23 seasons for the Baltimore Orioles, setting defensive career records for games, putouts, assists, chances, double plays, and fielding percentages among third basemen. A clutch hitter, Robinson hit 268 career home runs. He was the American League's Most Valuable Player in 1964 and the World Series MVP in 1970 when he hit .429 and made a variety of sparkling defensive plays.

What's the first thing a third baseman needs?

Concentration.

I think, first of all, when you talk about fielding, there's a lot more concentration that goes into it than most people think. You always hear it takes a lot of concentration to be an outstanding hitter. Well, it also takes a lot of concentration to be an outstanding fielder.

What do you concentrate on when the pitch is thrown?

You see the pitcher out of your peripheral vision. You don't look at the pitcher throwing the ball because you might not have time to follow the ball from the pitcher to the hitter and then react if the ball is hit to you.

At third base, you've got to watch that guy swinging the bat. You have to be ready for the ball to be hit to you because often it will get to you quickly because you're so close to the hitter.

How do you get ready to field the position as the ball nears the batter?

I've always been a proponent of moving a little from one foot to the other, in kind of a rhythm. But when you're doing this, you don't want to commit yourself to going left or right. You want to be balanced so you can go either way, depending on where the ball is hit. You want to end up in your rhythm squared up to the hitter, on the balls of your feet, when he's swinging that bat.

I liken it to tennis players on the receiving end of a serve. They always have a little movement with their feet, bouncing a little back and forth. I just think that's the best way to do it.

Where is your glove as the ball is hit to you?

When I signed in 1955, the Orioles could see I could catch the ball. I was an outstanding defensive player then. The one thing they told me, though, was that they wanted me to get my glove to the ground a little quicker rather than going down with the glove at the last second to catch the ground ball.

You start with the back of your glove almost down on the ground, with the palm facing up. And the glove pocket is open. You start that way not only for a ground ball, but for a bouncing ball too.

What's your body position?

As the pitch was thrown, I was down, bent over a bit, already flexed at the knees.

Why is that the best fielding position?

You have to go down to catch most balls anyway. If you're standing up straight to start with, then you have to take time to go down.

Most of the balls I would miss, or any kids would miss, go under the glove. You start with the glove down because it's much quicker for you to come up with the glove to catch a ball that hops up than it is to go down for a ball that stays down.

I started laying the glove on the ground almost. And I'd watch the ball go right into the glove.

When you're fielding a ball, you want to have your rear end down to help you **read the ball** better. Your hands are out in front of you. You don't want them too far out in front, or too close to your body, but just in a nice comfortable position in front of you.

Do you reach for the ball with just the glove hand?

You want to get your bare hand down with your glove hand when you can. I tried to catch the ball with two hands. That way I felt I could get the ball out of my glove quicker to make a throw.

What are the mechanics of throwing to first base?

You always want to step toward wherever you're throwing. So when you're throwing to first base after fielding a ground ball, you step toward first base and let it go.

How do you hold the ball?

When I took that ball out of my glove, 99 times out of 100 I had it gripped across the seams. Throwing across the seams will give you better action on the ball. It goes straighter and truer that way.

When do you move your feet to point yourself toward first base for the throw?

As you're catching the ball and positioning it in your hand to throw it, you're setting your feet to throw. It doesn't always happen that you can do that. It depends on how the ball gets to you and how you can field it, but I tried to get myself in position to throw as I caught the ball because that helped me get rid of the ball really quickly. I always felt that was one of my biggest assets.

What arm angle did you use to throw the ball?

When I could I threw overhand rather than three-quarters. That way the ball carried better and wouldn't sail.

How is playing third base different from the other infield positions?

Third base is a reflex position. Balls can get to you in a hurry. You can knock a lot of balls down, keep them in front of you, then pick up the ball and still throw guys out.

It doesn't work that way at shortstop, where you've got to catch the ball cleanly most of the time to get the batter out at first.

How does the third baseman make the play on a bunt? With the bare hand or with the glove?

If the ball is stopped or coming to a stop as you get to it, that's when you barehand the ball. But if it has a pretty good roll to it, that's when you have to field it with both hands.

On those rolling bunts, why have the bare hand next to the glove as you reach down for the ball?

You have to take into account that on that play, you're running in to get the bunt. If you reach down and field the ball with just your glove hand to pick up the ball, it's going to take an extra half step or another step to get your right hand into the glove to get the ball and throw it. That can mean the difference between the runner being safe or out.

What's your body position as you field the bunt?

When I first broke into the majors, they always told me to get in the best position to make a quick throw to first base after getting the ball. On the last couple of steps, as they get close to the ball, some players veer around the ball a little bit to give themselves a better throwing angle. But I think that may be overrated. I wanted to get to the ball as soon as I could and then throw it across my body quickly.

Where were your feet as you fielded the bunted ball?

Any time I picked up a bunt, my left foot was always forward a little bit. I reached down and picked up the ball with my left foot on the ground, and then with my next step I was able to throw the ball to first, pushing off on my right foot. If you come in and pick up the ball with your right foot forward, then you have to take that extra step to get your feet in position to make a throw.

How do you make sure your footwork is in the proper order to do that?

As you're coming in to get a ball, you might have to do a bit of a **stutter-step** along the way, just to get in rhythm to field the ball with the left foot forward.

What kind of throw do you make?

You have to throw on the run when fielding a bunt.

When I picked up the ball barehanded I would come up and throw over the top. But if I fielded it down low with both hands, I'd throw it from down there. I know a lot of third basemen throw from down low however they get the ball, but I felt I got more on my throw if I threw over the top.

The thing is, you have to learn to throw from every angle because you'll field balls in a lot of different body positions. If you field a ball with both hands low, you have to learn how to throw sidearm accurately.

How can you tell if someone is going to try to bunt for a hit?

In the big leagues you get a handle on who can bunt and who can't. So if you know a guy can bunt, you get right up in his face.

But even if you don't know a hitter, sometimes you'll see something that will give him away. You can concentrate and look closely for signs that he might be bunting. Maybe he's standing at the plate a little differently. Maybe the bat isn't back as far as normal, for instance. Sometimes the hitter might even take a peek at you to see where you're playing.

If I knew a guy might bunt for a hit, I'd move way in, get in his face, letting him know, "If you want to get a hit, you'll have to hit it by me. I'm not giving you a bunt hit."

How is it different on a sacrifice bunt?

There are times when you know the other team might try a sacrifice bunt because of the situation in the game. In those cases, you really creep in.

You have a couple of things on your mind in this situation. If the ball is bunted hard, you might have a play at second base. If it's a good bunt, you'll throw to first base. You have to know who's running and how fast they are. That will help you make a decision about whether you throw to second or first after fielding a sacrifice bunt.

What about a swinging bunt?

Those are more difficult because they come as a surprise. The batter takes a normal swing and the ball rolls down the line like a bunt. You're probably playing deeper when this happens. So, consequently, you just have to go after the ball, field it, and throw it to first as quickly as you can.

How do you make a play going toward the third-base line?

That's a play you have to make on the backhand, and it's probably the toughest play for a third baseman.

You just don't see the ball to your right as well as you do on a play going to your left, where you can pretty much see the ball right into your glove. To make the backhand play you're reaching back across your body.

On this play, I didn't like to run after the ball and then just make a stab at it with my glove. I wanted to get the glove out there toward the line and in position to catch the ball as soon as I could.

Once you field the ball on the backhand, how do you make a throw to first?

The throw on that play all comes down to the positioning of your feet.

When you catch the ball you want to get your feet in position to make the throw. That's the key. It's not just how strong your arm is. Usually when you backhand the ball you have a longer throw to first, so you want to stop, plant your feet, and make the throw. That's when you really want to get on top of the ball.

Of course, you can't always do it that way. I had a play in the 1970 World Series where I went 4 to 5 feet into foul territory to backhand a ball hit by Cincinnati's Lee May. For some reason I just got the ball, turned, and threw. It took one bounce and got Lee out at first base. I don't think I ever made that play like that but one time in my life.

I decided as I was fielding the ball that that was probably the best way to get him. If I had stopped and planted I don't think I would have thrown him out. Doing it that way enabled me to get rid of the ball a little quicker even though I wasn't trying to bounce the throw.

What kind of range does a third baseman need going to his left?

I always took everything I could get to. But you have to know where your shortstop is playing on certain hitters. The shortstops like you to cut balls off if you possibly can because it's a quicker, easier throw for the third baseman going to his left than if the shortstop has to field the ball going to his right.

How does the third baseman start a double play?

When you see the ball coming to you in a double-play situation, you try to get in position with your feet and body so you can face second base to make the throw after you field the ball. You try and give the second baseman a throw a little above his waist so he can turn the double play.

How do you track pop-ups?

I tried to catch the ball above my head instead of down by my waist because I felt like I could see it better than way. I always used two hands. I got under the ball as quickly as I could.

If the ball was close to a dugout or a fence, I might take my eye off of it for an instant to look down and see where I was, but the key is to get over to the ball as quickly as you can instead of drifting over to it for the catch.

★★★ YOUTH BASEBALL MEMORIES ★★★

I used to throw golf balls and tennis balls against the steps and field them. That gave me practice on **short hops** and pop-ups. I loved to play, that's all.

When I was in eighth grade in Pulaski Heights Junior High in Arkansas, I wrote a booklet called "My Vocation" about what I wanted to do when I grew up. I wrote that I wanted to be a professional baseball player, what with the hours they had and the pay they had. I put a lot of pictures in there. That was my dream. I think my love for the game overrode everything else.

When I was 14 to 17 years old, I played American Legion ball. I played on a lot of good teams. I think we had 12 or 13 guys who signed professional contracts. We traveled a little, going to tournaments in Memphis and Oklahoma. I played second base my last two years of Legion ball.

When I was younger, I played on a team called the Franklin Paint Bulldogs. We were known as the "Yankees of the Little League" because we always won. I can still see the article they wrote about us.

I knew the history of the game. I kept a scrapbook. When Babe Ruth died in 1948 I remember cutting out the story and pasting it in the back of my scrapbook. And when Grover Cleveland Alexander passed away I cut that story out and put it in there. I knew a lot of the players.

The Cardinals were my favorite team. They came through Little Rock every year and played an exhibition game against the White Sox right before the season started. I'd get out of school every year to go see them play. I never saw a real Major League game until I got to the big leagues.

We used to get the Cardinals games on radio. I listened to Harry Caray. That's why I was a Cardinals fan. Stan Musial was my hero.

I went to the largest high school in town, Little Rock Central, but we didn't have baseball. We had basketball, football, and track. None of the larger schools had baseball. I ran track just to get in shape for baseball season.

We had **pickup games.** I think there's a certain instinct you gain just by playing pickup games, when everything is not so structured.

★★★ BIG-LEAGUE MEMORIES ★★★

I played in York, Pennsylvania, in my first year of professional baseball. I played 100 games, hit .330-plus, did real well in Class B. So when the season was over the Orioles called me up. I was 18, playing in the big leagues. The Orioles weren't very good back then.

During my first big-league game against the Washington Senators I got two hits off Chuck Stobbs and knocked in a big run. I can remember running back to the hotel after the game and calling my mom and dad.

I said, "Hey, mom, dad, guess what? First big-league game I got two hits, knocked in a big run." I said, "Man, this is my cup of tea. I don't know why I was down in York."

And then I went 0 for 18 after that for the rest of the year. It was a pretty good lesson to learn. I knew these guys were way ahead of me.

As a youngster you dream of signing a professional contract, you dream of making it to the big leagues and winning a World Series, a championship, that's what it was all about.

With the Orioles, we had a good shot to win in 1960 and 1964, but didn't quite make it. In 1966 we accomplished all of those things. I always say that's my fondest memory. We were the World Champions. There are a lot of guys, real great players, who never played in the World Series.

I was a World Series MVP and an All-Star Game MVP, but the accomplishment I look at as my favorite one is being the MVP of the league in 1964 because that was something you did over the course of the 162-game, regular-season schedule.

I think it was Lee May who named me the Human Vacuum Cleaner after that play I made on him in the 1970 World Series. Lee came over to the

Orioles a few years later, and he still gives me the needle, saying, "You know what, Robinson? No one would have heard of you if I hadn't hit you that ball. You're lucky I hit them to you."

Defense was always a big part of my game. When people think of Brooks Robinson they think about the 16 Gold Gloves I won. They don't think about offense at all. I negotiated 23 contracts, and I never had a general manager say to me, "Well, how many runs did you save?" It was always how many hits did you have, how many home runs did you hit? Everything is evaluated on offense. Every sport is the same.

Defense gets overlooked a lot. But if you get good pitching and good defense, you'll win a lot of baseball games.

★★★ SUPERSTITIONS ★★★

I didn't really have superstitions.

But I did go through some routines. I had one game glove and others that I'd break in all the time. I could use the same game glove for two and a half years. I had my game bats, and I'd take them out of the bat rack and put them in my locker after the game.

MENTAL EDGE

As the batter steps into the batter's box, the third baseman goes through a mental checklist.

First and foremost is the situation in the game. What's the score? What inning is it?

The answers to those questions filter into the equation that will tell him where he should be playing as the pitcher looks in for the signal.

He knows it's a close game in the final inning. So he quickly runs some more questions through his mind. Is this batter a fast runner? Does he like to bunt for a hit? Is he good at it? Or is he a power hitter?

For a good bunter, the third baseman will move in a couple of steps, onto the grass, giving him a better chance to charge a bunt and make a play. As soon as he sees the batter's hands separate on the bat—an indication he's about to bunt the ball—he will be charging.

For a power hitter, he will back up and move a step or two toward the third-base line. That move, guarding the line, makes it more difficult for the hitter to get a ball past the third baseman just in fair territory, decreasing the chances of a potentially damaging extra-base hit.

This time he elects to play in on the grass. The batter's hands separate on the bat. The third baseman charges. The bunt is dropped down, and the third baseman is right there, pouncing on the bunt as if he knew it was coming. And he did.

—S. K.

GLOSSARY

Pickup games: Neighborhood games in which kids often choose up sides to pick teams. Not necessarily games in an organized league.

Range: The amount of ground a fielder can cover well going to the left and to the right.

Read the ball: To watch the ball carefully, so you can judge where the bounces will take it.

Short hop: A bounce so close to a fielder or the catcher that he can't catch the ball with his glove before it hits the ground.

Stutter-step: A shortened stride with a short, choppy step.

★★★★★★★★★★★★★★★★★★★★★★★★★★★★★★★★★★

TOM SEAVER

★★★★★★★★★★★★★★★★★★★★★★★★★★★★★★★★★★

National Baseball Hall of Fame Library, Cooperstown, NY

Elected: 1992
Position: Pitcher
Born: November 17, 1944, at Fresno,
California
Height 6-1; Weight 210
Threw and batted right-handed

Tom Seaver was a power pitcher who helped transform the New York Mets from lovable losers into a World Championship team. "Tom Terrific" won 311 games with a 2.86 ERA and 3,272 strikeouts in the National League. He fanned 3,640 overall, including 200 or more hitters 10 times. He struck out 19 in one game. He was the National League's Rookie of the Year in 1967 and a three-time Cy Young Award winner.

How much working out should a youngster do if he wants to be a pitcher?

I would stay away from weight training and let the body mature. There's enough time in your life to begin to be specific about things like weight training when you get to be 18 or 19 years old.

The thing is, you have to know what your body needs to get ready to pitch. "Smith" is not like "Jones." Everybody's a little bit different. Your body and its needs change through the course of your career, depending on how far you go.

How do you begin warming up before a game?

The biggest thing is blood flow. Just get your engine warmed up, get the blood flowing through the system before you start to put any stress on it.

How do you get the blood flowing?

You can do that by running, just raising your heartbeat, maybe jogging around the outfield. But don't warm up and then go sit down for a while.

Let's say it's a one o'clock game. You want to be finished with all your warm-up procedures by 10 minutes to 1, so you can give yourself 10 minutes before you go into the game. Around 12:25 you would do your jogging to get your heart rate up. You want to warm up for 15 minutes, so you want to start your throwing process by 12:35.

You also want to give yourself enough time to do some stretching with your legs and your shoulder, all those stretches that you're going to need.

You want to develop a system that works for you. It may change over a period of time, but you want to get yourself into some sort of rhythm because that helps you physically and mentally. Player A may need 12 minutes to warm up; Player B may need 17 minutes to warm up. Whatever works for you. You have to find your own system.

Once you start throwing, what pattern might you follow?

Personally, here's what I would do. With the exception of the last five or six minutes, all I was doing was throwing, just trying to get loose. Don't try to hit corners when you're not ready to pitch. Pitching and throwing are totally different.

How are throwing and pitching different?

Throwing is taking the ball from Point A to Point B. That's all you're doing. Pitching is when you're trying to put the ball in a certain spot.

153

So how did you mix the two in your warm-up process?

I would go to the outfield and throw long toss, throwing at a decent distance so I could stretch out my arm. I wanted to reach out, get the blood flowing.

Then I'd get on the mound, and for the last five minutes or so, that's when I'd throw my pitches, try to hit some corners. That's when I worked on my **release point.**

Are there certain pitching mechanics that come into play here?

You want to keep the elbow above the shoulder and the wrist above the elbow, in succession. That's a general rule. You do it this way because you want to throw the ball from **top to bottom** to get backspin and movement on the ball. Everybody's going to be a little different as they throw the ball, but the wrist joint has to be above the elbow joint unless you're a **submarine** pitcher.

How do you grip a baseball?

There's a pressure point on the baseball that you pitch off. Not everyone uses the same finger to put that pressure on the ball. Some throw off the middle finger, some off the index finger. (Hall of Famer) Nolan Ryan threw off the middle finger. I threw off the index finger. My index finger always went on the seam.

How do you know what works best for you?

You develop your own individual system just by throwing the ball. You can learn how to make the ball move in different ways just by putting pressure on the ball in different spots or holding the ball slightly differently.

On those days when you're not pitching, fiddle around with grips while you're playing catch with your buddies. Throw with the seam, across the seam. Try middle finger pressure, index finger pressure. Turn the ball. Throw with the thumb on the side of the ball, thumb on the middle of the ball. Watch the ball rotate as it comes out of your hand.

You can teach yourself. What's that pitch doing? Where did that come from? How did I hold it? Don't forget how you held the ball each time, remembering, though, that Player A is going to be different from Player B.

What are some basic grips for the various pitches?

You may have two different fastballs, the two-seamer and the four-seamer. On the two-seamer you place your fingers on the two small seams at the top of the ball. On the four-seam fastball your fingers are across the seams.

What difference in movement might you get from the two-seam and four-seam fastballs?

The two-seamer will sail or sink. The four-seamer will be what we call a riding fastball, a pitch that will take off at the end with late movement. You can learn how to make the pitches move in various ways by putting pressure on the ball in different spots as you hold it and let it go, or by holding it a little differently.

What about holding the ball for other types of pitches?

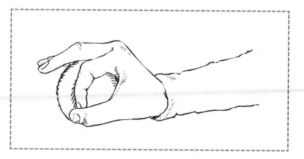

A curveball grip depends on the individual. Same with the slider, which has more of a hard, late break to it. Some pitchers grip the ball with the big loop of the seams on the back side, some on the front side. It depends on finger size and hand size and which finger you're putting the most pressure on. Again, you have to experiment to find what works best for you.

The changeup for me was a **circle change**. I'd hold the ball deep in my hand, but I would take my pressure finger off the ball. Once I had my index finger off the ball I could throw a changeup.

I would throw it just like I threw my fastball. The motion was "fastball," but the ball didn't come out traveling as fast because I had taken my power finger off the ball.

Where should you stand on the rubber?

Wherever it's comfortable for you.

I stood way over on the right side, as you face home plate. That's where I felt I could get the sharpest angle to the plate. If I was on the left side, my sinker would tend to be flat. You have to decide what works for you, where you can stand to make your pitches the most effective.

What you're shooting for is late, sharp movement as the pitch enters the hitting zone. You don't want to see it move when it's 45 feet away because then it's easier for the hitter to adjust to it. You want a slider, for instance, that will move late and down, 4 to 5 inches at the most.

How important is consistency in the delivery of each pitch to a pitcher?

It's very important. You want to make sure you can make the same pitch when the count is 1-and-2 and when the count is 3-and-2 with the bases loaded. That's the key. You want to develop to the point where you can throw any pitch that will work in the situation. When it's 3-and-2 and the bases are loaded, you don't want to be forced to throw the fastball. You want to have confidence that you can throw your slider to the outside corner, even if you're under pressure. That makes it tougher for the hitter.

What are some of the mental aspects of the craft?

As a pitcher, you have to know how to throw first-pitch strikes, get the first hitter out in every inning, and pitch inside. Those three things are A, B, C to me. If you don't do those things, then nothing else you try will work.

Talk about throwing strikes.

Just be confident in yourself that you can throw a strike. You're not going to do it all the time, but you want to throw a high percentage of strikes.

I'm not saying, "Okay, I'm going to throw this down Broadway, right down the middle of the plate." I'm saying you want to make a good quality pitch, inside or outside. If you're able to do that with three different pitches, or even two different pitches, you'll be in good shape.

Why is it vital for a pitcher to throw a first-pitch strike?

It's so much better to pitch ahead in the count because you limit what the hitter can be looking for, and you put him on the defensive.

If the batter sits there and can hit 2-and-0, 3-and-1, 3-and-2, you're giving him three chances to hit when his meter is in the green as opposed to in the red. Put him in the hole. Throw that first pitch for a strike.

Why is it equally vital to be able to pitch inside?

When a hitter knows he has to defend against the inside pitch, that opens up the entire plate for you. But if you don't throw inside, if he doesn't have to defend inside and he only has to defend on the outside corner, then he's ahead by 50 percent.

So you want to open up the entire strike zone for yourself. And you use the fastball. You don't have to throw a fastball for a strike on the inside of the plate. You can throw it off the plate inside. Even though it may not be a strike, you're sending the message to the hitter that you will throw the ball inside. You're telling him, "I'm not throwing at you. I'm throwing the ball 4 inches off the plate inside. And you're going to have to defend against that."

Why is getting the first batter to make an out such a big goal for a pitcher?

That's the most important out of the inning. You've got to focus on him and get that first hitter out. It's not going to happen all the time, but if you do that a high percentage of the time, your success rate will be much better.

Why? Because if you can get that first out, you can then get out of any inning with one pitch. If there are guys on first and second, boom, you can get a double play with one pitch and you're out of the inning. Pretty simple, but very true.

If you don't get the first hitter out and the other team puts runners at first and second with no outs, you can get a ground ball to shortstop for a double play, but now you've still got a man on third base.

This is not rocket science. The science is keeping focused and understanding that it isn't really very complicated.

What can you learn from watching a hitter?

You watch the hitter's weight balance, which way it goes.

If I'm facing a hitter for the first time, what do I do? I throw the ball off the plate, away, whatever side he's on, by maybe 4 or 5 inches. I don't watch the ball, I specifically watch the hitter and where his weight is going. I want some information before I attack him.

Is his weight going into the front of the plate, or is he pulling off the ball? Is he going out to protect the outside corner as a hitter? Is he pulling off inside, looking for a ball inside? Is his weight coming off the plate or going across the plate? Do his hands come through or go back? When you answer those questions, you've got something to go on.

It's a cat-and-mouse chess game. As a pitcher I want information about his balance.

What do you do with that information?

If he's pulling off—this is where the deception comes in—I'll throw a pitch inside the plate, off the plate. He'll foul that pitch back. Then I can pitch him away because I have him looking inside.

If he's bringing his hands quickly through the zone, I can throw a pitch that looks like a fastball but is not; I might throw a changeup. Then, all of a sudden he's committed, with his weight and energy all going forward, not letting him get any power behind his swing.

If a hitter keeps his hands back and waits and waits, he's susceptible to hard stuff inside because he has reduced the time he can get to the ball inside.

You're not always right, but you want to have a **game plan.** Also, you have to be honest with yourself about what you have to work with. A situation may call for a high fastball past the hitter, but if you don't have that good high fastball today, you may have to find something else that will work for you in those circumstances.

What role does the lower body play in the pitcher's delivery?

There's a school of thought in baseball that the lower half of the body doesn't have anything to do with throwing a baseball. I totally disagree.

My theory, and I don't have any computer printouts to prove it, is that you're taking the ball with your arm and moving it from Point A to Point B, trying to generate as much energy as you can to get rid of the ball. The rest of the energy is absorbed by the bottom half of your body where your big muscles are—your rear end and thighs—as opposed to the smaller muscles in the elbow and the shoulder.

And if the back leg has nothing to do with the power of the delivery, then why don't boxers stand straight up, with their back knee locked? They don't, because keeping their knees flexed generates power.

How would you define pitching?

Pitching is like dancing. It's rhythm and tempo.

Pitching is getting parts of your body into a certain position with a high degree of repetition. You have to figure out what makes everything work together. It is like a puzzle.

There are things you have to do that are key pieces to that puzzle. To me, it was leg lift that was important. I had to make sure I didn't rush my bottom (right) leg when I finished. That was my key.

I made sure I got my left leg up all the way into my chest and started the rhythm of my delivery. Everything has to work in great timing. If my left hand moved too early, then my upper right side was going to be late and I'd be flying open. That affected my control.

The worst thing to worry about is your arm. Your arm will go where the rest of the body goes.

How can kids learn from watching big-league pitchers?

There are two ways to observe pitchers whether you're watching a big-league game, a college game, or whatever. You can cut the pitchers off at the waist, watching the bottom half of the body and then the top half.

You also can cut the body into quarters: cut the pitcher right down the middle and off at the waist to look at him. Then you look to see what each component does.

Look at the non-throwing arm. What is it doing? What is the left leg doing? What is the top right doing? They're all coming together for the delivery, but what is each component actually doing?

What are some specific things to look for?

If a right-handed pitcher's left elbow points down, then his right shoulder is going up, which is good. If he's doing that, then he's throwing the ball from top to bottom, increasing his angle in delivering the ball to the plate.

If you have a chance to film yourself, take a good look. What is your bottom leg doing, the one that pushes off the rubber? You want to incorporate the thigh and rear end muscles. What is your landing leg doing? Do you have the flexibility you want?

How low should you be in pushing off the rubber? How much flex in your knees?

You don't have to get as low as I did or as low as (Hall of Famer) Nolan Ryan did. My right knee would touch the ground. But to me, there has to be some flexibility pushing off, using your lower body to get the **drive** off the rubber. There has to be flexibility in the front leg too.

Theoretically, you're going to generate "x" amount of energy to move the ball from point A to point B. And you get 70 percent of the energy on the ball itself.

Where does that other 30 percent go? It has to be swung back into your body. You created it. It doesn't disappear. It goes back into your body. Do you want it to go into your elbow and shoulder? Or do you want it to go into your thighs and your rear end, where you can absorb it better?

Should every pitcher use this method?

I'm not saying everyone should throw the same. Body type certainly has something to do with it. There are different degrees for all of this. Not everybody has to be the type of pitcher where the knee hits the ground and you drive off the rubber this way. If that's not for you as an individual, fine. But to me there has to be some degree of this incorporated in delivering the ball.

How do you pitch from the stretch position?

It's all individual how you set up in your stretch. But you have to remember one important thing. What's the primary objective? Throwing the baseball, that's what. That's primary.

If you're so worried about the baserunner that you're throwing bad pitches and you give up a double to left-center, well, you may have kept the runner at first base from trying to steal second base, but now he's either at third base or he scored on that double. So you won the battle, keeping him from stealing, but you lost the war by making a bad pitch because you were too concerned with the runner.

What don't you want to see when you look over at the runner?

You don't want the baserunner to get a **walking lead** because that might make it easier for him to steal. In your mind, you establish a maximum distance you'll allow the runner to get off the base.

If you can make the runner stop, keep him from taking that one extra step in his lead, then if there's a base hit, that one extra step may be the difference at home plate in the runner being safe or out on a bang-bang play.

How can you keep him from stealing or taking too big a lead?

If he goes too far, then you chase him back by throwing over. You can also hold the ball, just stand there in your stretch position. You can step off the rubber too, to chase him back.

The best defense is to have a catcher with a great arm. If you can make the runner stop, not give him a walking lead, your catcher will have a better chance to throw him out if he goes.

How difficult is it, as a right-hander in the stretch position, to see the runner?

You can practice using your peripheral vision. Your vision is not just 180 degrees; it's much more than that if you're aware of it.

You can always move your head to look at him. But you don't want to turn and open up your shoulder. You want to set in the stretch so you can be delivering the ball quickly to the plate. Remember, the first objective is getting the hitter out.

What role do the feet play in a pickoff move?

You have to be really quick with your feet on the throw to first. The feet get you in position to make a quick, accurate throw.

What is the slide step that some pitchers use in the stretch position?

In the slide step, you have a lower leg kick and a shorter stride to the plate so you have a quicker delivery to home plate.

How do you feel about using the slide step?

There's no way you can get the same amount of power on the ball with a slide step that you can get when you incorporate the bottom half of the body in your normal delivery.

How careful do you have to be when you make a pickoff throw?

How many times do you pick somebody off? Very rarely. So don't make a bad throw and give the runner second base or third base. Don't give him a free pass. Just make him stop.

How do you try to pick off a runner at second base?

What's the objective? It's the same as at first base. Don't give him a walking lead. If he's going to run, make him run from a standing start.

And how many times do you really pick a guy off second? Just don't throw it away. Throw the ball hip high on the inside part of the bag to whoever is covering.

You spin and throw. You have to step back off the rubber unless you lift your left leg (as a right-handed pitcher) and go to second base, which you can do. I used to spin to my left, but you can spin around the other way if you're quick enough.

Do you ever pitch around a hitter if there's a base open?

It depends on the situation and who the hitters are.

I tried to define in the last nine outs who I wasn't going to let beat me. Who was the most difficult hitter for me that day? I'd get rid of him, that is, I wouldn't give him a good pitch if that individual came up in a situation that could hurt me.

How would you do that?

If he was going to hit the ball, he was going to have to hit a perfect pitch. If I ended up walking him, fine.

There's a fine line there. If you pitch trying to protect against your mistakes, that's when everyone seems to make mistakes. But I'm not talking about **guiding the ball.** You have to know what your objective is. You might want to throw pitches two inches off the plate inside or two inches off the outside, pitches on the fringes. If he wants to swing at those pitches, fine.

But if you've got a runner at second base, and you're a right-handed pitcher and you've got a left-handed hitter up, you have a game plan for him. If he wants to hit the outside fastballs I'm going to give him to left field, fine. But I'm not going to give him a pitch he can drive into the alley in right-center.

Are there any last messages about pitching you'd like to offer?

If there's one important thing, this is it. And it's so simple. Don't deviate: throw hard stuff in, soft stuff away, hard stuff up, soft stuff down.

You want to keep the hitter off balance, break the hitter's timing. And you can break that timing by adding or subtracting velocity on your pitches.

Also, remember that a pitcher has three things to use. Three things, and three things only. Velocity, movement, and location. That's all there is. The pitch is going to go at a certain speed, it's going to move when it gets there, and it's going to go to a certain spot. Velocity is considered the most important these days, but in reality it's less important than movement and location.

★★★ YOUTH BASEBALL MEMORIES ★★★

Two of my biggest memories are from Little League baseball. I remember lying about my age, telling them I was nine and not eight because you had to be nine to play. They wouldn't let me play. I wasn't old enough. I was bawling like a baby.

In Fresno, California, where I grew up, we had a chalk line as an outfield fence. I remember my father coming to a game and walking around the outside of that line with my dog, a cocker spaniel, who was my pal.

Little League baseball was more than just the game, it was the innocence of youth, it was your mother and father following you. I can still hear my mother yelling encouragement.

I didn't play varsity baseball in high school until I was a senior. I grew and developed physically very late. I played Jayvee baseball when I was a junior, but my love of the game kept me playing.

★★★ BIG-LEAGUE MEMORIES ★★★

My first game was in 1967, against the Pittsburgh Pirates. It was the second game of our season. I was 22 years old. I had been in the Marine Corps, I'd been in junior college, and I had been a year at the University of Southern California.

I pitched six or seven innings that first game and got a no-decision. Woodie Fryman was pitching for the Pirates. I got an infield hit for my first Major League hit. I beat him to first base on the play. Chuck Estrada got the win that day, but I got my feet wet. I'm sure I felt nervous, but once I got to the mound I was okay.

The second game I pitched was in New York, against the Cubs. And that was the beginning of "graduate school" for me. I gave Billy Williams what I thought was a good pitch. He hit it off the right-field wall.. I had never had that happen to me before. Oh, my. Uh, oh. The rules have changed, I realized.

I knew I had to take my game to a different level. I won the game. I can't recall exactly what happened in every inning, but I can remember that the biggest lesson was Billy Williams's double. That was the beginning of the big league maturity process.

I was so nervous in the All-Star Game in 1967 it was unbelievable. The All-Star Game that year went 15 innings.

Tony Perez hit a home run off Catfish Hunter in the top of the 15th, and there were only two of us left in the National League bullpen, Claude Osteen and myself. And the phone rang. Claude had pitched two days earlier, so I knew the call was for me. I was a year and a half removed from USC, and I looked like I was about 14 years old.

I looked in the outfield and there were (Hall of Famers) Willie Mays, Henry Aaron, and Roberto Clemente. I was feeling better already.

I was coming to a new understanding about myself. It was a big emotional, intellectual step for me, because I was extremely nervous. Who wouldn't be? All these great players. You pinch yourself. You wonder, what am I doing here?

The educational process, the learning process, kicked in. When I got to the mound I realized that I knew what I was doing and I wasn't nervous anymore. I know this, I told myself. I may not know it the way I'm going to know it in 20 years, but I know it. I know what to do out here.

I knew who the hitters were. I knew it was (Hall of Famer) Carl Yastrzemski hitting second. It was a 2-1 ballgame, and once I got to that little round piece of dirt and on the rubber, I wasn't nervous anymore. "This is my classroom, and I know this stuff," I told myself.

I get two fly balls for outs on right-handed hitters, Tony Conigliaro and Bill Freehan. Now Yastrzemski comes up. I'm a rookie pitcher. I throw him four sinkers down and away, ball one, ball two, ball three, ball four: go to first base. A walk.

I know there's a right-handed hitter on deck, Ken Berry. And I know he's the only pinch hitter left. Before I'd left New York, I'd talked to Mets pitching coach Jack Lamabe who was a teammate of Berry's in Chicago, and he'd said, "If by chance you get to pitch to Ken Berry, he can't hit a slider down and away."

Bingo. Information locked in. Yaz up? Go stand on first base, stay over there. I'll walk you. And then three pitches to Ken Berry, two sinkers in and then a slider away—strikes one, two, three—see you later, a strikeout to end the game.

The thing is, every time you go someplace you can learn something about yourself or something new about your trade.

There's another story I remember. I'm in Chicago, an old-timer, 38 years old. Dave Duncan, the pitching coach for Tony LaRussa, is standing behind me as I'm warming up at old Comiskey Park.

I'm down to three minutes left in my warm-up, and he's standing behind me, saying, "Geez, Tom, you don't have a thing tonight." I handed the towel I was using back to him and I said, "It won't make any difference. I'll figure something out. It doesn't scare me." That's the fun part of it. I won that night.

★ ★ ★ SUPERSTITIONS ★ ★ ★

I don't know that you'd call them superstitions, but I had routines with my sleep, diet, and exercise. I did crossword puzzles or found someone to play bridge with to take my mind off my start that night before I went out to warm up.

I would just do things to get myself ready. I had this whole system to make everything feel comfortable.

But one Tuesday I get to the ballpark. I'm scheduled to pitch on Wednesday. So I still have time for running, sprints, whatever, being consistent with my routine. I walk into the clubhouse and pitching coach Rube Walker hands me the ball and says "You're pitching." And I said, "No, I'm pitching tomorrow."

He says, "No, you're pitching tonight." And I said, "No, I'm not ready to pitch tonight." He said, "You're pitching tonight because scheduled starter Jon Matlack was in a car accident on the way into the park. It wasn't anything serious, but he banged his knees and is sore and can't pitch."

So he gave me the ball. I told him again I wasn't ready to pitch. I was out of my routine. I wasn't scheduled to pitch until the next night. Well, I pitched a two-hit shutout and struck out 14 that night, so there went my theory about needing the routine to be ready.

The one superstition I had was not stepping on the foul line. I don't know where that came from. I haven't the slightest idea. Maybe I went to a game and saw someone else do it. I used to just step over it.

MENTAL EDGE

While every pitch and every play ultimately can have a major effect on the outcome of the game, the pitcher-batter confrontations best embody the sport as a chess match. Each pitch is as much a mental exercise as it is a physical exercise.

And because the pitcher is holding the baseball, no action begins until that pitch is delivered to home plate. But before the pitch is thrown, the pitcher's mind is racing faster than the speediest fastball, taking note of numerous factors.

What is the batter doing? Has he edged closer to the plate, possibly looking for an outside pitch? Has he moved up in the box, possibly looking for a curveball? What pitch got him out the last time? How good is my breaking ball today? Do I trust myself to be able to hit my spot with it on a 3-and-2 pitch with runners in scoring position?

The answers to those questions factor into the equation that determines which pitch might be thrown next, as well as the location.

—S. K.

GLOSSARY

Circle change: A changeup in which the thumb and index finger form almost a circle in the grip.

Drive: To hit the ball with authority.

Game plan: A plan on how to pitch to a certain hitter.

Guiding the ball: Trying to aim the ball to a particular point, as opposed to just throwing it with confidence.

Release point: The position of the arm and hand when the ball is thrown to the plate.

Submarine: A pitching motion in which the arm is about waist-high, or even a little lower, and parallel to the ground when releasing the ball.

Top to bottom: If you think of a clock, it's like starting at twelve o'clock and moving down to six o'clock.

Walking lead: When the pitcher is in the stretch position, the baserunner walks off his base, trying to keep his momentum heading toward the next base.

OZZIE SMITH

Elected: 2002
Position: Shortstop
Born: December 26, 1954, at Mobile, Alabama
Threw right-handed, batted both

Ozzie Smith was nicknamed "The Wizard" for revolutionizing defensive play with his acrobatic fielding style. He was a 15-time National League All-Star. He earned 13 Gold Gloves. Smith accumulated 2,460 hits, stole 580 bases, and helped the St. Louis Cardinals reach three World Series, including their title-winning 1982 appearance.

What's special about a double play?

For me, the double play is one of the greatest plays in the game because you can get two outs for the price of one ground ball. The pitcher can be struggling, but that's when the ground ball truly becomes his best friend.

The improvisational part of turning double plays has always fascinated me because there were many times when I didn't know how I was going to turn a double play. How I physically turned it was determined by where the runner was.

There was creativity in turning double plays. That intrigued me and was one of the things that allowed me to turn as many double plays as I did in my career.

When runners are on base and you are anticipating the possibility of a double play, what other factors do you consider as the shortstop?

A lot has to do with who is at the plate. You certainly have more time with some guys if they are slower runners.

One of the factors is whether or not the pitcher is a ground-ball pitcher. That comes into play. If he throws sinkers or keeps the ball low, there's a good chance you'll probably get a ground ball.

Where do you position yourself at double-play depth?

If the runner at first is a guy who doesn't run very well, then you know you have a little bit more time to turn the double play because he won't be on top of you right away at the bag. That allows you to play back some, which gives you a little more range in fielding the ball.

But if you have a guy you know can run on first base, even an average runner, then you have to cheat in a little bit, maybe three or four steps from normal depth.

As shortstop you should be able to position yourself so your glove hand will be in line with the ball because it's an easier play going to your glove hand than it is going away from your glove hand.

Is turning a double play all about the strength of your arm?

A good infielder should have good, quick feet. You need to be able to get yourself in a good position to throw. Quick feet give you the ability to go straight up in the air and the flexibility to throw to first, in spite of the fact that the runner is right on top of you, trying to stop you from turning the double play.

How do you turn a double play started by the second baseman (the 4-6-3)?

There is no book that says you have to do it a certain way. That's the improvisational part I'm talking about.

Sometimes you might reverse the **pivot** to turn the double play because of where the runner is sliding. Sometimes you get to the bag at the same time the runner does, and you have to be able to use the bag as a springboard to get up in the air and throw to first base. Ultimately it's about getting two outs when you get a ground ball.

People always said to me, "You're not supposed to throw off the right foot." Well, who says? I never allowed those things to interfere with my ability to complete a play, and the completion of the play is what's most important.

How do you get to the bag on a 4-6-3 double play?

You want to get there as quickly as you can but with your body under control. That's the operative word, control.

Where do you want to be when you turn the double play?

The bag is your protection from the runner. You don't want to be too far on the right-field side of the bag because the runner can get to you there.

The closer around the bag you turn the double play, the safer you will be because you can use the bag as protection from the sliding runner. I always tried

to arrive in position behind the bag. When you come across the bag going toward first base as you make your throw, you're opening yourself up to injury, because now the runner is coming down on you and his job is to slide into you and **break up the double play.**

When do you tag the base?

I always made sure I kicked the bag when I had the ball in my hand. It's very easy for people to cheat and get the ball and be past the bag. Well, to me, that's not a double play. Umpires have been lax about calling that, giving you the out even if you're not on the base when you have the ball, and their excuse is that they are protecting the players.

172

But you're supposed to be on the bag when you catch the ball, not after you catch the ball. And it always burned me up when people said to me I wasn't on the bag. If you watched me, I'd say 99.9 percent of the time I touched the bag when I had the ball in my hand.

In general, talk about the "feed" to the person performing the pivot on the double play.

As the shortstop, when you're feeding the ball to your second baseman, you don't want to hide the ball. You want to make sure he can see it all the way.

Also, my job as shortstop is to get the ball to the second baseman as quickly as I possibly can in an area where he can do what he has to do to turn the double play. I, as the shortstop, don't want to determine how he has to turn the play. His safety might be in jeopardy if I give him a **feed** in an area that puts him at risk of the runner sliding in.

If I'm performing the pivot, his job is to get me the ball at second base as quickly as he can so I, as the shortstop, can determine what I'm going to do with it.

That's the only predetermination. I have to get the ball to him as quickly as possible, and the second baseman has to get the ball to me as quickly as possible. Then the pivot man can do whatever it is he has to do to avoid the runner and avoid serious injury.

When you feed the second baseman for a 6-4-3 double play, do you throw the ball to him overhand or underhand?

Your momentum and where you catch the ground ball will determine how you feed the ball to the second baseman.

What type of throw will you make on a ground ball to your left?

If you're going toward the bag when you field it, it's much easier to feed underhand. And when you do feed the ball to him this way, you have to make sure that you stay down with your body. If you come up with your body as you make this type of feed, the ball has a tendency to go higher than you want it to.

So when you throw underhand, you throw the ball on a line, and you should

do what I call following your throw. That is, you turn and face the second baseman and you don't stop your momentum, you take another step or two toward him after you've released the ball. That helps get him the ball quickly and accurately.

What happens if the throw isn't on a line?

If you throw the ball too high in the air, it slows the second baseman down because he has to reach up for the ball and then pull it down to make a throw. That extra time may allow the runner to beat the **relay** to first.

Also, if you throw it too high in the air, it gives the runner from first base an extra step or two to get to the second-base bag, and that might make it easier for him to break up the double play.

How do you start a double play on a ground ball hit to your right?

Any time you're going away from the bag it's a lot tougher play. In a normal double-play situation, where you're able to get in front of the ball, you go down with your body and hands to catch the ball, and you don't want to come up when you make the throw. Again, if you come up to make the throw, you're giving the runner more of an advantage.

So you learn to do things in one motion. I catch the ball low, with my right foot planted. Once I've done that, the hard stuff is all done. I've gotten to the ball and I'm in position to throw to the second baseman at the bag. My feet are what puts my body in position to throw to whatever base I want to throw to.

In one motion I pivot on the balls of my feet, facing the second baseman and making a throw from an overhand or three-quarters motion.

Do you throw to second for a double play the same way you'd throw to first base for a routine out?

No. It isn't a throw where I use a "long arm." I'm not bringing my arm way back to make a throw.

This kind of throw is like throwing darts, using your wrist to make the throw. It's not rearing back and having the great arm. Guys with great arms want to show them off all the time, but for this type of throw—turning a double play—everything has to be done very precisely, very quickly.

Where do you throw the ball?

You learn generally where your second baseman likes the ball to turn a double play. Some like it over the middle of the bag. Some want it over the center-field side of the bag.

Most of the guys like the ball about chest high. My job as the shortstop is to throw it in that area as consistently as I possibly can. You don't want to throw it at their shoe tops or over their heads because that will make it tougher for them to turn the double play.

What do you do in a rundown as a fielder?

When you have a runner trapped between bases and you have the ball, you want to run with the ball up in your bare hand, right up by your right ear if you're a right-handed thrower. You don't want to be holding the ball with your hand down by your side because then, when you have to make a throw, you have to bring it all the way back up near your ear to throw it. And that costs you time.

What type of throw is best in this situation?

It's like throwing a dart, a flick of the wrist. But you want to make sure you're holding the ball so the person you're going to throw it to can see it. He doesn't want to be surprised by the ball coming out of nowhere.

Which direction do you want the baserunner going in?

You try and get the runner's momentum going back to the base he started from. Sometimes you do that with your first throw.

Let's say the runner began running from second base and is trying to get to third. The shortstop has the ball. The third baseman—in this case the guy who is receiving that first throw—might take a step toward the shortstop so he has momentum going toward the runner. That will help you **close up the rundown.** It shouldn't take that many throws to get the runner.

The first guy with the ball is the guy who gets the runner out of control, forcing him to commit to running one way or the other. Once that happens, it's easier for the guy making the play on the other end of the rundown to tag him out.

What does the defensive player have to be careful of in a rundown?

You want to make sure you don't create interference.

A good baserunner who gets picked off is going to be adept at finding a way to bump into you after you've made a throw. If there is contact, the umpire can call interference, which would make the baserunner automatically safe, giving him a base.

So you want to run in the baseline with the ball by your ear so you can flip it to the person you're throwing it to, and then you want to peel out of the baseline so there is no contact with the runner.

And what you do is follow your throw. If you've thrown to third, for instance, you follow your throw by running to third base, backing up the person who just received the throw. And now you're in line at third base to receive a throw if the rundown continues.

★★★ YOUTH BASEBALL MEMORIES ★★★

I never got drafted out of high school. There weren't any great memories other than my love for the game, enjoying what I did.

Often I played games by myself. I'd throw a ball over the peak of a roof, trying to be fast enough to run around to the other side and catch it. It was the determination I had as a kid that helped enhance my skills as a professional athlete.

I do remember one of my most exciting moments when I was 12 or 13 and first started playing organized baseball. I grew up in Los Angeles, and I lived across the street from the Manchester Recreation Center. I had just gotten my new uniform and I didn't have the outer socks, the socks that are called the stirrups. My mom worked, and I knew that on her way from work she was going to stop and get me the outer socks. I can remember how excited I was when she came to the park and she had those stirrups for me.

The thing is, you've got to love what you're doing. I tell young people if money is your driving force you're never going to get the most out of whatever it is you choose to do. If you don't have a true love for what you're doing, you're probably doing the wrong thing.

Baseball gave me the opportunity to do what I truly loved doing. When I was going to go to college, I had to do some real soul-searching because basketball was what I enjoyed doing more than anything else at the time. That's what I excelled at in high school.

But in doing that soul-searching, I realized baseball was what I loved doing. I had great hand-eye coordination and I had speed. All I was looking for at that point was an opportunity.

(Hall of Famer) Eddie Murray was on my team in high school. That's where the scouts' attention was. I didn't have a lot of size. I didn't hit the ball out of the ballpark, so I had to take a different route to the big leagues.

I went to Cal-Poly at San Luis Obispo for college because they gave me an opportunity to play baseball. I began on a partial academic scholarship. I didn't get a partial athletic scholarship until I was a sophomore.

★★★ BIG-LEAGUE MEMORIES ★★★

When you play 19 years, there are a lot of great memories, such as being traded to St. Louis in 1982 and playing in a World Series, then hitting a home run in the playoffs in 1985 and winning another World Series that year. That game-winning home run off the Dodgers' Tom Niedenfuer (in the bottom of the ninth of the deciding Game 5 of the National League Championship Series) got us into the World Series.

I actually had to learn how to hit at the big-league level. I wasn't an accomplished hitter when I got there. And in 1985, understanding what I had to do offensively came together for me. I knew exactly what type of hitter I was going to be. I had learned how to take that inside pitch and hit it down in the corner.

That's all I was trying to do in that playoff game. The Dodgers had been pitching me inside, and I wanted to hit the ball into the corner to get myself into scoring position.

In that particular instance, the pitcher supplied the power and I supplied the technique. You get that moment in time. I wasn't trying to do anything extra. I wasn't trying to do anything more than I had done all year, but that was my moment in time. I certainly was not a home run hitter. (The homer was the first in 3,009 left-handed at-bats for the switch-hitter.) I was just trying to hit a ball in the corner, and it happened to go into a place where the ball carried out of the ballpark.

I guess my trademark became the back flip I'd do before the first pitch of a game. I was a bit reluctant to do the first one because I didn't want to be tagged as a **hot dog.** I took the game much too seriously, so I didn't want that to happen.

The first time I did it was for the San Diego Padres, on the final day of the 1978 season. The Padres weren't very good back then, and it was Fan Appreciation Day. They had 50,000 people at the game. It was an exciting day. The Padres knew I could do it, so they asked me if I would because it would be a way to get the fans excited.

Lo and behold, they liked it enough to ask me to do it again on Opening Day in 1979. So it became my trademark, and now I have little old ladies coming up to me all the time saying, "We know who you are. You're the guy who does the flip." So I guess it turned out pretty well.

I got drafted in 1976 by the Detroit Tigers. They offered me $8,500. I told them if they gave me $10,000 I would sign. They said, "No, we can't do that." So I went back to school, and being the good businessman I was, I got drafted by the San Diego Padres in 1977. I signed for $5,000 and a bus ticket to Walla Walla, Washington.

★ ★ ★ SUPERSTITIONS ★ ★ ★

For me, Hamburger Helper was one of my favorite meals, and when I'd hit one of those bumps in the road over the course of the season where things weren't going so well, I'd fall back on Hamburger Helper. My wife would fix me Hamburger Helper when I needed to get back on track. Psychologically, or whatever, that would get me going.

MENTAL EDGE

Teaching a shortstop how to turn the double play isn't all that difficult. He gets to the bag, receives a throw from the second baseman, or first baseman, or pitcher, and quickly throws the ball to first base for the double play. Most of the time, he receives a nice, chest-high throw from the other infielder.

But the shortstop knows it's not all that easy. Obviously, there are some footwork issues that have to be practiced. One of the biggest lessons, though, is that you can never anticipate a good throw.

Nice, routine chest-high throws are not made all the time. When they are, those are the easy ones to turn. Those can be turned almost in your sleep if you have had enough practice and experience.

But how about those throws at your ankles? How about the throws that skip to you on a short-hop? How about the throws you have to jump off the base to corral?

Ah, now you're talking creativity and concentration. Now you're talking about finding a way to complete the double play, not settling for the one out on a bad throw that increases the degree of double-play difficulty.

You don't want to do anything silly, mind you. There are some times when it's only possible to get the one out at second base. Because of a bad throw, you just feel fortunate to have gotten that one out.

But when the shortstop can jump up for a high throw, come down on the bag, and throw to first as he hits the bag, completing the double play, his satisfaction level can't be much higher.

—*S. K.*

GLOSSARY

4: Second baseman.

6: Shortstop.

3: First baseman.

Break up the double play: To slide into the fielder turning the double play, knocking him down so he can't make the relay throw to first.

Close up the rundown: To shorten the distance between the defensive players.

Feed: The toss from one fielder to another to get an out at a base.

Hot dog: A player whose flamboyant antics on the field go beyond the bounds of proper baseball etiquette.

Pivot: The turn on the double play.

Relay: The throw from second to first on a double play.

★★★★★★★★★★★★★★★★★★★★★★★★★

DON SUTTON

★★★★★★★★★★★★★★★★★★★★★★★★★

Elected: 1998
Position: Pitcher
Born: April 2, 1945, at Clio, Alabama
Height 6-1; Weight 185
Threw and batted right-handed

The right-hander was a model of consistency in his 23-year career, winning a total of 324 games, striking out 3,574 batters while pitching for the Dodgers, Astros, Brewers, Athletics, and Angels. Sutton was a four-time All-Star, reaching double figures in wins in 21 of his 23 seasons. He pitched in four World Series and authored five one-hitters.

What is the difference between
"pitching" and "throwing?"

People who are blessed with good arm strength and good bodies can just rear back and **fog it**—throw it as hard as they can all the time. That's "throwing."

I think "pitching" is disrupting what a batter hopes to accomplish. In its simplest sense, pitching is trying to keep the batter from doing what he wants to do. Or it's allowing him to do it the way you want him to do it, so you can get him out.

What was the most valuable lesson you ever learned about pitching?

When I was a 12-year-old Little Leaguer, my sixth-grade teacher, Henry Roper, taught me that it was important to throw strikes and that the most important pitch was the fastball, but that you needed to locate the ball, put it in the spot where you wanted it.

Once you could locate that pitch, then the lesson was to be able throw something other than the fastball if you were behind in the count, to keep the batter off-balance.

That, in essence, is pitching. You try not to give in to what the hitter wants you to do. You try to stay one thought ahead of him, watching what he does.

What can you learn from the hitter before you even throw a pitch?

Most times a hitter with his first couple of swings will tell you what he wants to do.

If he waves the bat back and forth low, there's a pretty good chance he's a low-ball hitter. If he waves the bat back and forth high, there's a pretty good chance he wants the ball up. If his first move when the pitch comes is to open up, there's a pretty good chance he wants the ball inside. If his first move is to lean over the plate, there's a pretty good chance he wants the ball outside. If his bat's slow, he's an off-speed hitter. If his bat's pretty quick, chances are he's a good fastball hitter.

The late Don Drysdale used to say if you could see the knob of the bat as the hitter got ready to swing, don't try to come inside with a pitch because he'd be ready for it. If you couldn't see the knob of the bat, the chances were good he couldn't handle an inside pitch.

So pitching is garnering all the little tidbits like that, collecting information that can help you determine how you might want to pitch to each hitter, much like a scouting report you get in the big leagues.

How important is it to know what you can do on the mound?

You want to know what your assets are and use them to be the best pitcher you can be. I could never be a **power pitcher** like (Hall of Famers) Nolan Ryan or Tom Seaver. But I could be me.

What I thought I could do was hit a gnat in the butt with my fastball and throw strikes with anything else. I had good control. That's how I pitched.

The most important thing is to figure out who you are and what you bring to the park.

How do you change what you do as you keep advancing, facing tougher and tougher competition?

One of the great mistakes young pitchers make is that they'll dazzle through the minor leagues and then get to the big leagues and think, "Oh, man, I've got to throw harder, I've got to be finer."

You still have to pitch the way you are the most successful.

Is there one pitching delivery that works best?

When we teach young pitchers, especially in pro ball, we get into the unfortunate habit of trying to put them into a mold. We try to have everybody pitch the same way, instead of looking at them and seeing what might work best for each individual pitcher.

A pitcher is an outfielder with a windup. He's an outfielder throwing to the plate with a windup, that's all he is.

How can you figure out what delivery might work best for each individual?

If you bounce a ball to a kid 30–40 feet away and tell him to throw, he'll show you his natural **arm slot** instinctively as he makes his throw. That's the greatest foundation right there. You figure out where his arm slot is and then you give him a windup or a pitching motion that makes him comfortable, and then you teach him to throw strikes.

How important is it to mix your pitches, throwing breaking balls and changeups in addition to fastballs?

There isn't a person around who can throw a hundred consecutive fastballs and not get hurt by the hitters. Most people can hit a fastball eventually. So mixing pitches helps you disrupt the hitter's timing, which he needs to hit the ball well consistently. Good hitting is about having your right timing and being in the right groove. Good pitching is about throwing the right pitch and keeping the hitter off balance.

What does "throwing strikes" mean? Just firing a pitch over the middle of the plate?

When I talk about throwing strikes, I'm not talking about throwing pitches belt-high down the middle. I'm talking about throwing quality strikes, pitches on the corners of the plate, for example. There's a difference.

It's like comparing the terms "control" and "location." A guy can have good control and throw strikes all night long and not have good location. Location is putting the ball in the most vulnerable part of the strike zone for each hitter, taking the sting out of his bat, so even if he hits it, he won't be able to **drive** the ball. That's what I mean by a quality strike.

For instance, there are some guys who are low-ball hitters, so you don't want to throw a low pitch right down the middle to them. Some guys can hit inside pitches, so you want to throw down and away to them. Any pitch thrown in the right spot is a good pitch.

Much is made of the intense pitcher-batter confrontations and strikeouts. Is it wimpy to get a guy out on one pitch?

Part of that mindset is our ego. And part of it is that we have done a poor job of schooling kids that it's okay to get an out on the first pitch. You hear pitchers say, "I've got to make him miss the ball." But that's just macho stuff, baseball's version of trash talk.

If a guy wants to jump on the first pitch, throw him a pitch he can hit, but don't throw him one belt high and on the inner half of the plate. Take a little off that pitch. Give him a little changeup, a little curveball, or a slider, something that's near the plate.

Aggressive hitters are easier to get out than patient hitters. He might hit your pitch, but he probably won't drive it because you have disrupted his timing, and you'll have an out on one pitch. Aggressive hitters will hit your mistakes farther, so it's a bit of a double-edged sword. That goes back to keeping your pitches out of the areas around the plate where you, as a pitcher, are most vulnerable.

Which is more important for a pitcher, the ability to use his brain or his arm strength?

I have seen very few brain-dead heavers make it to the Hall of Fame.

A brain-dead heaver is a guy who throws at 99 miles an hour and doesn't think. Usually those guys grunt loud, reach back, and fog it. The catcher doesn't have to stick down signs because the guy is just throwing fastballs. The catcher just has to get ready to catch the ball.

Some pitchers have done that, but there isn't anybody alive who throws hard enough to get by only on one pitch. That's why changing speeds on your pitches and having information about the hitters can help you, especially if you don't throw at 99 miles an hour.

Pitching, to me, was so much fun because it's a chess game. It's a battle, but it's not always the guy with the biggest **cannon** who comes out on top. Maybe it's the guy with the best placement of his defenses. Maybe it's the guy who thinks one move ahead. Maybe it's the guy with the smartest catcher. I always felt pitching was so much easier when I had a catcher who thought like I did, who realized the **battery** is an equation of two people and not one.

What is the key to fielding the position?

The best thing you can do after you deliver the ball is to get back on balance.

How concerned should you be about fielding the position before you throw the pitch?

The pitcher's first job is to make a quality pitch. His second job after that is to become the fifth infielder. If you reverse the priorities, you find yourself giving up home runs instead of singles.

If your primary objective when you throw is to get in a good fielding position, then there's a pretty good chance you're going to be backing up third base a lot. That's because you won't be making a quality pitch, and the batter will be hitting the ball in the **gap** somewhere.

Is there one follow-through every pitcher should adopt?

Everyone has an innate natural delivery. Once you complete that delivery, then you do what you can to help defensively.

I used to end up on the right side of the infield because my follow-through took me toward first base. But finishing your delivery in a certain spot doesn't mean you can't still be a good-fielding pitcher. It just changes the area within which you can do your job.

I always felt that any ball hit from the middle of the rubber to first base was mine to go after. I felt I did a good job there. The third baseman had to take care of the other side of the infield because I fell off to the first-base side.

How do you field bunts?

When you go after a bunt, you go under control.

You have to know the situation. You may have to make an adjustment in your delivery so you can get over to field a bunt along the third-base line. You have to be aware of who the runner is at first so you know how much time you're going to have to make a play when you field the ball.

You also have to trust your catcher. He has the play in front of him, and he makes the call where you're going to throw the ball. If he yells, "second, second, second," don't question it, just turn and throw the ball to second base after you've fielded it.

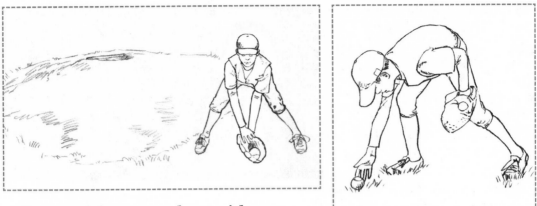

Do you pick up every bunt with your bare hand?

Always go for the ball planning to use your glove and your other hand. Let your instincts take over after that in deciding whether to use just your bare hand.

If the catcher calls "second," how do you make the throw there?

If you're a right-handed pitcher, when you're making a throw to second, turn to your left. It's quicker and you'll get more on your throw.

How about on a routine grounder back to the mound with a runner on first and less than two outs? How do you start a double play?

You want to know who's covering the bag, whether it will be the shortstop or the second baseman. You should know that before the pitch because you've checked with your fielders.

If it's a double-play ball and the second baseman is covering, lead him with your throw, aiming about a step to the right side of the bag as you look at it. If the shortstop is covering, lead him a step to the left side of the bag. That way he can catch the ball, quickly find the bag, and throw to first for the double play.

What kind of throw do you make?

You see a lot of guys throw **lollipops** to second. If you do that, your shortstop or second baseman is going to get knocked into left field by the sliding runner.

So you want to make a good, firm throw. And you try not to be off-balance when you make the throw. The key, though, is to make sure you get at least one out, the one at second base especially, because then you'll be getting the lead runner.

If you are able to field the ball cleanly, you're going to have time to turn, look, and throw, and let your teammates take it from there.

What are the techniques for covering first base on a ground ball hit to the right side?

I was taught to run diagonally to a spot two steps shy of the bag and then turn toward the bag and run parallel to the first-base line. That way you could catch the ball, hit the bag and then turn toward the inside of the diamond. That got you out of the way of the runner, and if there is another runner on base, you can quickly check to see what he is doing.

This all goes back to knowing—on every pitch—what you're going to do if the ball is hit to you or somewhere else on the field. I was taught that lesson as a 12-year-old.

Doesn't a pitcher's brain get cluttered with so many things to think about?

When you are a pitcher, a lot of things are going through your mind until you get set in your delivery, ready to throw the ball to the plate. Then, the only thing that should be in your mind is making a quality pitch.

You can't control whether the ball is going to be hit, you can't control how hard it's hit, you can't control if it's going to be caught, you can't control if it's an out. What you can control is devoting 100 percent of your energy to making a quality pitch.

★ ★ ★ **YOUTH BASEBALL MEMORIES** ★ ★ ★

Camaraderie wasn't a big deal to me. I just wanted to play, I just wanted to pitch. I played other positions only long enough to find out I was no good at them. There wasn't a market for a shortstop like me who couldn't run, throw, field, or hit.

But I loved pitching because the whole game revolved around it. Nothing happened until I threw the ball. And if I threw it well, we could score fewer runs and win. I loved the responsibility that went with being a pitcher. That was a joy. That responsibility was fun. That's how I felt when I was 12.

I've had college and high school teammates say they thought sometimes I looked down my nose at them because I was playing a different game from them. I didn't mean to, but I was playing for a different purpose than they were.

I was playing baseball to get to the big leagues. When I was 12 years old, I wanted to pitch in the big leagues. When I was 16 years old, I wanted to win 300 games. I wanted to make the Hall of Fame when I found out there was one.

If you want to play tiddledywinks, you play tiddledywinks. You want to skip rocks on the lake, fine. But at 12, baseball became a job to me, and I had fun doing my job.

The fun was being able to do it. That was the satisfaction. Fun was throwing against the wall. Fun was catching pop-ups. Fun was just playing catch. But when I got on the mound, pitching became my job. My job was getting the batter out.

I started practicing pitching in September of 1957. I'd throw a ball off the wall. My sixth-grade teacher taught me how to pitch. He taught me all the fundamentals that I used until the very last day I pitched.

I pitched a perfect game in my second start in Little League. Six innings,

18 hitters up, 18 hitters down. I pitched three no-hitters that first year and went 9-0.

But my third- or fourth-biggest thrill in my whole life was when I was a junior in at Tate High School, a little bitty high school outside Pensacola, Florida. We won the state championship, and I pitched a two-hitter for 13 innings. It was the first time we'd even been to the state tournament, and we won. That stands out because it was something we had never done and I got a chance to be a part of it.

★ ★ ★ BIG-LEAGUE MEMORIES ★ ★ ★

When I was with Milwaukee in 1982, we needed to beat Baltimore in the final game of the season to get to the playoffs. I got the chance to pitch that game. I would have felt deprived if I had not been able to be part of that. Robin Yount had some big hits that won the game, and I just happened to be out there for a few innings on the mound.

The mound was my office. I had a structure for my day. If a member of the media came by and I had a 7:30 game, we could visit until 6:30. But at 6:30, that's when the office door closed. It was time to go to work. And I wanted everyone to be as committed as I was.

One of my memories was when I won my 210th game, which broke the Dodgers record of Don Drysdale, one of my mentors. I won it sitting in the dugout. I gave up a home run, but Von Joshua won the game for me with a home run.

Drysdale was working for the Angels at the time. When I came into the clubhouse, the phone was ringing. Instinctively I knew the caller was Big D, and it was. He congratulated me. It was just a wonderful exchange.

I also remember my first start in the big leagues. A lot of people asked me if I was nervous, and I could honestly say I wasn't nervous because I'd already done it 10,000 times right here, in my head. For me that was as real as doing it that night.

The parallel I would use is if you study for a big exam, and you pass it, are you surprised? I'd been studying for my first exam for nine years, so it was fun to take the test.

It was against Houston, and I didn't win. I came out in the eighth inning, and a reliever gave up a home run and we got beat. I had given up one run. When I came out I was winning 2-1 and had a couple of runners on base. But when Ron Perranoski came in and gave up a home run, I ended up the losing pitcher.

My next start was against Houston in Houston, and it was against Robin Roberts, someone I admired. I had patterned my philosophy after him. I got more butterflies that night because I was going against Robin Roberts. That was goose bumps time, but I won that game.

★ ★ ★ SUPERSTITIONS ★ ★ ★

None.

I threw five one-hitters, and I carried no-hitters into the seventh or eighth inning a number of times. Everybody on the bench would be avoiding me as the baseball superstition dictates. I would go sit down and say, "Guys, I know I've got a no-hitter going, come on." They probably thought I was nuts. Maybe they were right. But no conversation in the booth or on the bench is going to break up a no-hitter. It's going to be the guy with the bat.

To me, there's a difference between routine and superstition. There's a difference in being structured. I'm the most structured person you'll know, more so when I played because for me it was all a matter of preparation. So if I had a superstition, it was that I wanted to be prepared.

When I left home, the last bit of advice I got from my dad—who grew up a tenant farmer, construction worker, and carpenter and who never missed a day's work—was this: When you get to professional ball, there are going to be a lot of people better than you. But don't ever let anybody be better prepared or outwork you. I didn't.

MENTAL EDGE

Up until the ball has left his hand, he is one thing: the pitcher.

He has been processing information all game long. What is his game plan for each hitter? What kind of stuff does he have? Does his fastball have enough pop to get him some strikeouts in crucial moments? Does he have to paint the corners all night? Why isn't the umpire giving him the low fastball on the inside corner?

All of this information, and much more, is floating around in the pitcher's brain between pitches. Then, as he winds up, all he's thinking about is making a quality pitch.

Once the ball leaves his hand, however, the pitcher becomes something else: the fifth infielder.

Automatically, he has to know what to do defensively. If there's a bunt, what part of the field is he covering? If he fields the bunt, which base should he throw to? What does he do on a ball hit right back to him?

And on a ball hit to the right side, the pitcher can't think. He just has to react, racing over to cover first in case the first baseman is going to make the play. If he forgets, the batter has a base hit and the pitcher is quickly in a jam because he fell asleep mentally.

—*S. K.*

GLOSSARY

Arm slot: The angle of the arm from which the pitcher releases the ball.

Battery: The defensive unit made up of the catcher and pitcher.

Cannon: A strong arm.

Drive: To hit the ball with authority.

Fog it: To throw the ball hard.

Gap: The space between the outfielders, called left-center and right-center, respectively.

Lollipops: Balls thrown softly and with a high arc.

Power pitcher: A pitcher who throws mostly hard, fast pitches, such as the fastball and slider.

CARL YASTRZEMSKI

Elected: 1989
Position: Outfielder
Born: August 22, 1939, at Southampton, New York
Height 5-11; Weight 185
Threw right-handed, batted left-handed

National Baseball Hall of Fame Library, Cooperstown, NY

An intense performer, Yaz played in more games (3,308) than any other American Leaguer, topping 3,000 hits and 400 homers. He was a three-time AL batting champion. In 1967 he won the league's Most Valuable Player Award, winning the Triple Crown: leading the AL in batting (.326), home runs (44), and RBIs (121).

What is your stance in the outfield as you get ready for a pitch?

Basically you want to get into a good athletic position.

I would say you want your feet to be shoulder-width apart, and you want your knees flexed, standing on the balls of your feet so you are ready to run if the ball is hit your way.

I also liked to have my left foot a little out in front of my right foot. It felt more comfortable for me to do it that way.

What are you thinking when you're standing all the way out there in the field, so far from the action?

I've always said it takes the same intensity playing in the outfield on every pitch as it does for a hitter getting ready for every pitch.

You have to assume the ball is going to be hit to you on every pitch. That's how you stay ready. You can't be thinking about your last at-bat or your next at-bat because that will take away from your concentration.

How does knowing the hitter help an outfielder?

If a right-handed hitter is a **dead pull hitter,** let's say, you might favor him down the left-field line a little bit. And maybe for a left-handed hitter you'd move off the line, more toward left-center if you knew that was where he hit the ball a lot.

That kind of thing was easier in the big leagues because you saw the same hitters year after year. You knew them, so you had a pretty good idea where they might hit the ball, and that could be an advantage.

How did you catch a fly ball?

If it's a routine fly ball, you always keep your eyes on the ball.

When I caught the ball, I always liked to catch it up around my face area. And I always wanted to come in on the ball as I made the catch, even on a routine play with no one on base, because I'd always be practicing as if someone was on base and I had to get ready to make a throw after catching the ball.

Did you catch the ball with one hand?

No. I always carried my throwing hand up with the glove when I caught the ball because that made it quicker to transfer the ball from the glove if I had to make a quick throw to get a baserunner.

I'd do this even on a routine play with nobody on. It

was a practice routine, so when someone was on base and he was going, you weren't left in the dark, all of a sudden having to make a throw. You had already been practicing it.

Did you keep your eyes on the ball all the time?

Almost all of the time. When you took off to the left to catch a ball in the gap or to your right, you kept your eyes on the ball.

The only time you took your eyes off the ball was on a ball over your head. That was a tough play. What you would have to do was run to a point where you thought the ball would come down and when you got to that point, you'd look up again, picking up the flight of the ball over your shoulder.

How do you become good at catching fly balls?

It's like becoming good at anything: repetition, repetition, repetition.

I can remember as a young kid, even back in Little League, I would go with my father and uncles, who were on a semipro team that played a couple of days a week and practiced three or four days a week. If there was a right-handed hitter up taking batting practice, I'd go to left-center and **shag** fly balls because that's where most of them would be hit. When a left-handed hitter came up, I went to right-center to shag fly balls.

Some of the best practicing you can do is to go to the outfield during batting practice and track down fly balls off the bat. That, to me, was better than having **fungoes** hit to me.

What are the mechanics of charging a base hit and making a quick throw to a base?

I had a great advantage because I played a lot of infield in high school and in my first year in pro ball, so charging ground balls for me was second nature.

If no one was trying to score, I always kept the ball in front of me if it was coming to me on the ground. I didn't want it to get by me and give anyone an extra base, so I'd play it safe and make sure I blocked the ball.

But when I was in left field, if someone was trying to score from second base on a hit to left, I would charge in for the ball. I would reach down for it, fielding the ball on my left side, not in front of me, so I could keep the same speed going when I picked up the ball.

Where was your bare hand during this pickup?

When you brought the ball up in the glove, the bare hand had to be there so you could get the ball out of the glove as fast as possible to make a really quick throw. If you did it this way it didn't take too many steps to get into your throwing motion.

What if the ball was hit toward the left-field corner?

On a play like that, you're probably trying to hold the runner to a single, so you want to get to the ball as quickly as you can. But you kind of take a rounded route to the ball so that as you get to it and backhand it, you field the ball with momentum, and you come up ready to make a throw to second base.

If you go to it at a straight angle, your back will be facing second base when you pick up the ball, and it will take a little more time to make a throw. If you round off your path, the front of your body is facing second base as you come up with the ball. This way you are in a better position to throw quicker and with all your power.

How did you hold the ball?

You want to grip the ball across the seams when you make a throw because the ball will carry that way and stay in the air. If you don't grab the ball correctly, it will tend to sink as it gets to the infield. If the ball is carrying well and you're throwing from a far distance, even if you can't reach the **target** in the air, the ball will bounce truer and straighter to the target this way.

You can practice the right grip just by playing catch. The more you do it, the more it becomes second nature. Eventually when you reach into your glove for the ball your fingers will go right across the seams.

Where did you aim your throw?

Whenever I threw the ball—warming up before a game or even in the outfield before innings—I would try to hit the guy I was playing catch with right in his chest. You have to practice that because that's where you want to throw the ball back to the infield on a play, in case the ball has to be cut off.

I'd always play catch with an outfielder because we would be throwing the ball farther distances than the infielders had to. That way you could stretch it out, lengthening how far away you were from the guy you were playing catch with, always throwing to his chest.

One of the most important plays an outfielder has to make is to try to throw out a runner trying to score. How did you do that from left field?

My first aim was to make sure I didn't take too many steps before throwing the ball.

After fielding the ball you want to come up to throw, trying to get rid of the ball as soon as you can. And when you field the ball, if possible, you want to be facing dead-on to your target, in this case, the catcher at home plate. Depending on how deep you are, you can either try to throw the ball to the catcher in the air or make a strong one-hop throw to the plate.

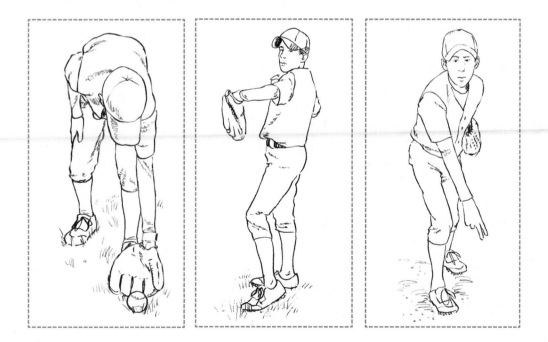

I would use my momentum coming in to help me make a strong throw. And I would let my momentum go to the target even after I let go of the ball. In other words, I didn't try to pull up and stop as soon as I threw the ball because I felt that little bit of extra momentum, maybe one or two more steps to the target, would help the ball carry.

What's the toughest play for an outfielder?

The line drive hit right at you because you aren't able to get a good perspective on the ball right off the bat. You can't tell right away whether it's going to take off on you or stay on a course where you don't have to go back for it.

Sometimes your first step might be in on a line drive, and then you can be in trouble if it takes off and goes over your head. You don't have time to catch up to it.

I used to practice that a lot. I'd have somebody hit fungoes right at me or over my head to help me develop better instincts for that play.

How did you track fly balls in the sun?

I wore sunglasses. And when the ball went up, I put my glove up to block out the sun, using it as a shield so I could see the ball without the sun affecting me.

Sometimes there would be what we call a "high sky." That's when there are no clouds. That's the toughest sun condition because if you take your eye off the ball for even a second or two, when you look back up to find it you might not be able to pick up the ball again.

Playing the sun comes with experience, just like playing the wind as a difficult condition. You should pay attention to the conditions during batting practice or before the game to help you with the conditions during the game.

When should you dive for a ball?

As an outfielder you have to know the situation of the game. There are times, depending on the score and the inning, where you might not want to take a chance and dive for a ball. But I always played very aggressively. If I thought I had a chance I'd try to make the diving catch.

I remember in the 1975 playoffs against Oakland, Reggie Jackson hit a ball to left-center and I dove for it. It was a base hit that landed maybe 30 or 40 feet in front of me and to the left of me, but I still dove for the ball and was able to cut it off, holding him to a single. That paid off because the next guy hit into a double play, which wouldn't have happened if I hadn't cut the ball off and held Reggie to a single.

★ ★ ★ YOUTH BASEBALL MEMORIES ★ ★ ★

I grew up in Bridgehampton on Long Island, New York. In Little League I played shortstop and pitched. I threw strictly fastballs. I had a great arm, threw some no-hitters, but I threw strictly fastballs.

I used to have a little plate and the strike zone painted on the side of the barn. I made the strike zone smaller than the normal strike zone so I could practice control. I'd throw tennis balls against the barn door, trying to hit spots. I was probably doing that when I was 9 or 10 years old.

I played in Pony League and American Legion as a shortstop and a pitcher. We came from a very small area. I think we had only 20 people in my Bridgehampton High School graduating class. But in American Legion we went to the semifinals in Maryland. When we went upstate to play in the playoffs I remember pitching a no-hitter and hitting a couple of home runs against a team from Syracuse.

We were allowed to play as freshmen because the school was so small. It was just a bunch of kids who could play. We had several kids sign professional contracts.

★ ★ ★ BIG-LEAGUE MEMORIES ★ ★ ★

One memory was a catch I made in 1967 off Tom Tresh in Yankee Stadium, saving a no-hitter at the time for Bill Rohr, even though he eventually lost it with two outs in the ninth.

That play was a definite run-to-the-spot and leap in left-center. And when I dove, I dove toward the fence, so I never picked the ball up until the last split-second, over my shoulder. In fact, I didn't pick it up until I was diving. I went to the spot, dove, looked up, and there was the ball.

It was very intense because the pitcher had a no-hitter going. That's an example of how anticipating on every pitch that the ball is going to be hit to me helped me out.

Of course, getting my 3,000th hit and 400th home run come to mind.

But a lot of my memories go back to 1967. My first six years, it was difficult to play in Boston because we were finishing last or next to last. But in that last month of the 1967 season, when we were fighting for the pennant with four teams, the competition made the game fun and made it much easier to play. And we won the pennant.

People would ask, "How do you take the pressure of that?" Well, let me tell you, pressure was when you were playing on a lousy team. When you were playing for a pennant, playing on a good team, there wasn't any pressure. It was fun, and it was easier.

That 1967 season changed the whole Red Sox organization from losers to winners. I can remember, even in the minors my first year, everything fed off the Major League team. In the late 1950s, the Red Sox were not so good, either. That filtered down to the minor leagues. You almost had a losing attitude down there.

My first six years with the Red Sox, we were lucky if we had 10,000 people in the seats on a Friday night. Then in the middle of 1967, when we were winning, the ballpark became packed every night when the fans realized we had a shot. And all of a sudden, baseball returned to New England.

Another thing I remember is that it took me a long time to get my 3,000th hit. It took something like 12 at-bats. I was trying to hit a home run, that's why. After the second game in which I went 0-for-whatever, Walter

Hriniak, the hitting coach, came up to me and said, "What are you doing? I know you're trying to hit a home run. Just get a base hit."

When I saw the hit go through the right side against the Yankees, I felt like, "finally." It was the last day of a home stand, and I wanted it to happen at Fenway Park. We were going on the road the next day. It wouldn't have been the same if it had come on the road.

The 400th home run was also at Fenway. I don't remember who the pitcher was, but the one thing I do remember is that when I hit the ball, I knew it was gone.

You knew when you hit one. There were only a few, especially at Fenway if the wind was blowing in, when you weren't sure. If you hit it and the wind was blowing in, you ran hard.

I remember hitting a ball against Detroit one day when the wind was blowing in. It was a damp, cool spring night, and Al Kaline, one of best right fielders ever to play the game, was playing right field. He didn't move. I thought the ball was up in the bleachers somewhere, so I started trotting. All of a sudden he started running, so I started running. The ball ended up on the warning track. I got a double, but it should have been a triple.

★ ★ ★ SUPERSTITIONS ★ ★ ★

I was very superstitious. I wore the same outer socks—the stirrups—for years and years. They had holes in them, but I wouldn't change them.

If I was hitting well I'd wear the same sweatshirt too.

MENTAL EDGE

What do I do with the ball if it comes to me?

The question arises in every level of baseball. And while the outfielders are viewed as having a boring defensive job, way out away from all of the action that takes place in the infield, that doesn't mean they don't have to ask themselves that same question each time the pitcher delivers a pitch to the plate.

They can be standing around all game, with nary a ball hit their way until the game is on the line. And they have to be ready.

The runner is dancing off second base. The game is tied. It's the bottom of the last inning, and there are two outs.

The left fielder knows what he's going to do if the ball comes to him on the ground. He knows that will mean it's a base hit. He knows the runner will be trying to score, and that, because there are two outs, the runner will be getting a good jump, off on the crack of the bat.

So the left fielder's job is simple. Catch the ball and throw it home.

He gets in his best fielding position and stares in toward the plate. He sees the batter swing. He sees the ball soaring over the infield, heading his way.

The ball bounces several feet in front of him. It's a base hit. The runner is heading home. The left fielder doesn't even have to look up to see that. He knows that's what's happening.

He keeps his eye on the ball. He knows he can't play this one safe. He has to charge the ball and hope he can field it cleanly so he can make a throw to the plate.

He accomplishes a clean scoop and uncorks a strong one-hop throw to the plate. The runner is dead meat, out by several steps. The game remains tied. It's going to extra innings.

The left fielder jogs in. Who says playing the outfield is boring?

—*S. K.*

GLOSSARY

Dead pull hitter: For a right-handed hitter, it's hitting almost everything to the left side of the field; for a left-handed hitter, it's hitting almost everything to the right side of the field.

Fungoes: Ground balls and fly balls hit by a coach during practice.

Shag: To catch balls during batting practice.

Target: Where you want to throw the ball.

ROBIN YOUNT

National Baseball Hall of Fame Library, Cooperstown, NY

Elected: 1999
Position: Shortstop
Born: September 16, 1955, at Danville, Illinois
Height 6-1; Weight 175
Threw and batted right-handed

Robin Yount was one of three players to earn a Most Valuable Player Award at two different positions. Yount, an everyday player in the big leagues at the age of 18, played shortstop and center field for Milwaukee, spending his entire 20-year career with the Brewers. He finished his career with 3,142 hits. As the MVP in 1982, he led the Brewers to their first berth in the World Series.

How do you get ready to field a ground ball? Is there one specific body position that works best?

You want to be in a good, comfortable position. It's similar to hitting. There are a lot of different ways to set up. But the key is to have both feet on the ground with the weight on the balls of your feet as the pitch is crossing the plate.

Are you standing still as the ball approaches the plate?

A lot of guys take a little hop as they get set in their pre-pitch routine, kind of walking into your fielding position. But you have to be careful when you do this.

Why?

You have to time the move right. I see a lot of guys still in the air when the pitch is crossing the plate. They're not down with their feet ready to go left or right, depending on where the ball is hit.

If you're not down in your fielding position, it may cost you a half-step on your **range,** which could be the difference between your getting to the ball or having the ball get by you for a hit.

How do you catch a ground ball?

First and foremost—to get as basic as you can—no matter what level you play, you have to keep your eye on the ball. It's as simple as it sounds. Yet, I've watched Major Leaguers take their eyes off the ball and miss it.

That becomes the single most important habit you need to develop, focusing on watching the ball go into your glove every time it comes your way, so that when it happens in a game, it's automatic that you don't take your eye off the ball.

What eye level works best for fielding grounders?

You try to keep your eye level as constant as you possibly can. Obviously, when you're running around chasing ground balls you can't keep your eyes exactly in the same place all the time. But you try as best you can.

How is that affected by your fielding stance?

You want to start in a position low enough that your head is not going way up or way down as you go after the ball.

If you get too low, though, then you can't go after the ball, or cover as much ground as you should. So you can't get too low. And you don't want to get too high, either, because then your head has to go up and down more than you would like, making it more difficult to watch the ball into your glove to catch it.

If your head is bobbing too much, your perspective on the ball isn't good. It will be tough to see all the hops well, which will make that grounder more difficult to catch cleanly.

How do you make the play in the hole?

Some people teach that you should surround the ball, which is running back in kind of an arc so you can catch the ball on your forehand side. I'm not a fan of that approach because it usually makes you throw off-balance and takes you a couple of more steps to make the play.

I think when you go into the **hole** the backhand pickup is the best way to do it.

The reason is, as soon as you've backhanded the ball, you've put yourself in a much better throwing position instantly. You reach for the ball across your body as your left foot lands, and as you catch the ball, you plant your right foot and throw to first.

When you backhand the ball, your whole body is closed, your shoulder is closed and **squared up** to the **target.** This way you can throw with your feet planted, under control, instead of throwing on the run or off-balance.

How do you make the play up the middle?

For a shortstop the hardest part of going to your left is the throw. It's awkward. You're going in the wrong direction—basically running toward right field—and you're throwing back against your body's momentum to first base.

You try to close up your left shoulder as best you can, which means turning that shoulder as much toward your target as you can. That's difficult to do in this case.

How does that affect the type of throw you can make?

Normally when you can close up your shoulder you can make a throw that will carry straight to the target. But this type of throw, because of your momentum, will tail a little bit. It will have a bit of a left-to-right movement. You have to adjust to that and account for it.

How do you account for the "tail" on the ball to make an accurate throw?

You pick a spot that is to the left of your target. In this case, your target is first base, so you aim your throw maybe three or four feet to the left of the first baseman as you are looking at him, because the ball will tail back to him with the left-to-right movement that comes with the sidearm type of release you have to make for this throw.

In general, how should you grip the baseball for a throw?

Ideally you try to hold the ball across the seams because the ball carries better and goes straighter. Whenever the seams are off-line, the ball tends to move.

That's why pitchers don't hold it across the seams very often unless they throw the ball exceptionally hard. Pitchers are looking for movement. But as an infielder or an outfielder, you want your ball to go as straight as possible so it can carry better and is easier to handle for the guy catching it.

How do you practice this grip so you can throw this way without hesitation?

Anybody who plays catch for a lot of years learns what this grip feels like without even looking into the glove after catching the ball.

You try to teach this to kids when they're young, and by the time they're 13 they should know how it works. In a perfect world, as you take the ball from your glove and you're getting into the throwing position, you're gripping that ball across the seams at the same time.

How do you field a chopper that is hit over the mound?

The mental side of the game comes into play here because before you ever even field or throw a ground ball you have to understand who has hit it and what kind of speed that runner has.

Knowing all of that determines sometimes, on slow-hit balls or choppers over the mound, how you make that play.

How does it matter if it's a fast runner or a slow runner who hit the chopper?

If it's a guy who can run fast, and he hits a chopper over the mound, let's face it, you don't have any time to read the hops or anything. You just charge the ball as hard as you possibly can. And if you have to try to barehand that ball and then throw it on the run, that's probably going to be your only chance to get the runner.

But if it's a slow runner who hits that same ball, then you have some time. That changes how you can make the play. You may be able to read the hop a lot better, give yourself a good hop to field, and still be able to throw out a slower runner.

So knowing the speed of the runner ahead of time is something that is critical to any good fielder because that determines how you play a particular ball.

What do you mean by "reading the hops?"

It means tracking the ball, watching it carefully from the instant it leaves the bat.

Why do you need to read the hops?

You always try to get the best hop you can as a fielder—the biggest bounce, the longest hop—because those hops are the easiest to catch, which means it's easier to make the play.

Then there are the ones we call "tweeners," the ones that are in-between hops. They're not long, easy hops. They're the ones that bounce about four feet in front of you, making it difficult for you to adjust to the way the ball will bounce as it nears your glove.

It's so difficult to react to any adversity in that hop—if it comes up a bit higher than you thought or stays down lower than you thought it would. You don't have time to react to something you don't expect.

What role do the feet play in a good fielding position?

Your feet are all part of putting you in the best position to field the ball properly. Most good fielders have good footwork, meaning they're reading the hops with their eyes, while they also are adjusting their feet to put themselves in the best position to catch the ball.

More often than not, if your feet are in good position, your body and your throwing motion will function much more naturally as you field the ball and make the throw. With your feet in position, your body will be under control when you field the ball and when you throw it.

What do you mean by being "under control," and how is that helpful?

By under control, I mean you're not off-balance when you're fielding or throwing. You try to avoid being off-balance because that's when you might make errors.

It isn't always going to be possible to be perfectly under control when fielding a ball or throwing it. That's why it's so important to watch the ball all the way into your glove. Even if you are off-balance and in bad body position, you're still probably going to be able to catch the ball if you focus and watch it all the way.

What does a shortstop do on cutoff plays?

Let's say there's a runner at first and there's a ball hit in the left-field gap. Then you know the runner is going to round third and head for home.

So as the shortstop, you go out in the cutoff position. You go out into the outfield a little distance, depending on how hard the ball is hit and how strong the outfielder's arm is.

You square up to the outfielder to give him a good target. That means your hands are up high, and you have your back to home plate, so you look as big as you can to him when he throws the ball.

As he throws the ball, you turn your body to get in a good position to catch the ball and relay it to third base or home plate, wherever the runner might be

going. As you receive the ball from the outfielder, your body is sideways, with your left shoulder pointed to your target, whether that's third or home in this particular case. You turn your body this way so you're in the best position to catch the ball and throw it all in one motion.

Do you catch the throw from the outfielder with one hand or two hands?

You catch the ball with two hands because you want to have a quick transfer of the ball from the glove to the throwing hand. So your glove is up and your throwing hand is right next to it as you receive the ball. You reach into the glove to grab the ball at the same time as you're moving to get into the best throwing position.

It's all a timing thing, so you can do it all in one smooth motion: Catch the ball as you land with your left foot on the ground, grab the ball out of the glove as you step with your right foot, and then throw, pushing off the right foot.

If your bare hand isn't near the glove when you receive the ball, then you have to bring the hand over to get the ball out, which may cost you a little extra time. Just that little extra time can be the difference between the runner being safe or out.

How aggressively do you pursue pop-ups in the outfield?

As a shortstop, you have to have the mentality that any pop-up hit toward left field or center field is your ball all the way, and that you are going to catch it at all cost until you hear an outfielder call you off. It's the outfielder's job to call you off and catch the ball if he can make the play, because it's easier for him coming in to get the ball than it is for you going out for the ball.

But if an infielder is looking for the outfielder ahead of time, expecting him to make the play, then he's going to have problems. He won't be pursuing the ball aggressively enough, and it may end up dropping for a hit between the shortstop and the outfielder.

Do you always keep your eyes on the pop-up?

When you're the shortstop, on the tough pop-up—the one that is way over the your head between you and the outfielder—you often have to take your eyes off the ball because you can't run as fast if you're looking at the ball all the way. You want to run to a spot where you think the ball is going to come down and then look up and pick it up again out of the sky.

What about on a more routine pop-up? Do you watch that one all the way?

You probably won't take your eye off the pop-up that isn't too deep into the outfield, which is one the outfielder probably can't get. It's not deep enough for you to have to.

In a perfect world, you try to stay behind the ball, run deeper than the ball might land and then catch it coming in because it's easier to come in to catch a ball than it is to have to drift out after the ball. Sometimes, though, because of the wind and conditions and the way the ball is hit, you might have to drift out after it anyway.

How is the center fielder the "boss" of the outfield?

They always say the center fielder has priority over anybody else on a ball hit into the gap. He's kind of the ringleader out there.

The left fielder and the right fielder have the same mentality on fly balls that the shortstop and second baseman have on pop-ups. That is, they go after anything in the gap with the mentality that it's theirs to catch until they hear the center fielder call it. It's the center fielder's job to call off the left or right fielder if he thinks he can make the play.

What angle should a center fielder take to track down a fly ball?

The angle you take to the ball depends strictly on how the ball is hit. There is no given angle to take. Ideally you want to take a straight line—not a **banana route**—from where you're playing to where the ball is going to land. If you can do that, you've certainly made it as easy as possible.

How important is it to check out the wind every inning?

You have to monitor the conditions constantly. You're always looking for flags or whatever to give you a hint about what the wind is doing because that will affect fly balls quite a bit. And if you're not aware of the wind, you can get fooled even on the simplest fly ball.

How does the wind affect where you might play?

When the wind was blowing out, I used to play a couple of steps deeper because anything hit in front of me was going to hang up a little longer than normal. So I could play a couple of steps deeper and still get to the ball in front of me.

If the wind is blowing in toward home plate, you can cheat in a couple of steps because the ball hit over your head is going to come back to you a little bit.

If the wind is blowing to the left or to the right, you can always cheat in the direction of the wind. For example, if the wind is blowing to your left, then you move a couple of steps to your left because anything hit to your right will come back to you in the wind.

How do you combat the sun?

You make sure you take sunglasses out there with you. If you don't need them, put them in your pocket. But don't go out there without sunglasses and then, when the sun comes out from behind the clouds later in the inning, lose a ball and say you should have had it.

You can also use your glove as a shield. As the ball goes up, you put your glove up to block out the sun.

But there are times when, no matter how hard you try, the ball is not going to come out of the sun for you to see. You can try to improve your chances of finding the ball, however. You're taught to catch fly balls right over your head so you can watch the ball into your glove, but the ball in the sun is a little different. You might have to play that one to the side a little bit so you can see the ball better. You're trying to keep the ball out of the sun from your line of sight by catching it this way.

When you're batting, after you've hit the ball, then what?

You always have to run hard out of the batter's box. You make doubles and take extra bases from your first two steps out of the batter's box, not by picking up the pace halfway down the baseline.

If you run hard out of the box you keep pressure on the defense. They know if they bobble the ball, you're always going to be in position to take the extra base.

How aggressively do you go down the line when you've hit a routine grounder to shortstop, for instance?

You want to run hard right through first base. Don't slow up when you get to it. And you want to hit the front of the bag, and as little of the bag as you can, because that's the shortest distance you can run and be safe. If you're hitting the back of the bag you're going farther than you need to, and that little distance could be the difference between being out or safe.

Do you look at the base all the way down the line?

I think about halfway down you should look at the front edge of the bag where your foot will hit.

How do you feel about sliding into first base?

I don't think you should slide into first base unless you're avoiding a tag.

I'm not concerned with your getting hurt sliding into the base because you slide into other bases too. I just don't believe it's faster to slide into first compared to running hard through the bag. And sliding makes it a lot more difficult for the umpire to make a call. I rarely see guys called safe on bang-bang plays when they slide into first.

How do you make the turn at first base?

As I said, I believe in hitting as little of the base as possible when you take your turn. You want to hit that inside front corner of the bag. Your foot can hit half dirt and half the corner of the base. Use the base as something to push off of to help you make a better turn.

Which foot should hit the base when you make your turn?

Ideally you hit the base with your right foot because doing so opens up your body to the next base.

But more important than what foot you hit the base with is that you hit the base on stride. To hit it on stride you always have to pick up the bag in your vision early. If you pick it up when you're halfway down the line, it's amazing how often it comes up on stride. When you look down at it late, that's when you tend to have to use a stutter-step to hit the base, and that costs you some momentum.

What's the key to taking an extra base as a baserunner?

You have to understand outfielders' arm strengths and be aware of where they're playing. That information will give you an idea of when you can take an extra base and when you can't.

You can take advantage of guys who don't throw very well or guys who are playing deep. You have to know all of that before the ball is hit. That's part of your thinking before you even take your lead.

How important is the third-base coach if you try to go from first to third on a base hit?

He can help out, but the longer you play the game the more you should understand on your own whether or not you can make the extra base, especially going from first to third. If you know ahead of time where the outfielders are playing and what their arm strengths are, you don't need any help to decide whether you're going from first to third.

When does the third-base coach become more important?

If you're trying to score from first on a ball in the gap, that's where your third-base coach can help.

What is a secondary lead?

When the pitch is made, as you read the play, you get a little bounce off, a step or two more, from your initial leadoff. The size of the secondary lead depends on how close the infielders are holding you, especially at second base.

When you take that secondary lead you want to be on the balls of your feet and you want to be landing on your front foot, your right foot, as the ball is crossing the plate so you're in good position either to run to the next base or get back to the base you're running from.

How aggressive should you be in taking a lead?

The situation in the inning and the game always dictates how aggressively or how conservatively you run the bases. If you're losing by a few runs late in the game, you might not want to be too aggressive. In that case you might want to wait for other things to happen offensively.

How do you read balls in the dirt, which can result in taking an extra base?

If you're really paying attention, you follow the flight of the ball out of the pitcher's hand. If you see that the ball is going to wind up in the dirt and short-hop the catcher, before it even happens you should be ready to go to the next base if that ball gets away from the catcher at all. Anticipation is all part of following the ball and not just looking at the catcher and waiting for something to happen.

★ ★ ★ **YOUTH BASEBALL MEMORIES** ★ ★ ★

My favorite Little League memory was when I was 12 years old. I was in an all-star game, and I went 4 for 4 and pitched a no-hitter for the Woodland Hills Sunrise Little League. That was my favorite game. That was a fun day.

When I was in high school, I was a big Joe Rudi fan. The Oakland A's were in their heyday at that time, and he played for the A's. I liked his hitting style. It's funny, he was a left fielder and I was a shortstop, but I still liked him.

Rudi was a clutch hitter, and I liked the way he hit the ball to right-center really well as a right-handed hitter. I ended up hitting with a fairly closed stance, which I'm sure must have come from him because he stood with a real closed stance. He was always the guy I watched the most all through my high school years. He visually influenced my hitting as much as anybody.

And that was funny because toward the end of my career, Sal Bando became the general manager for the Brewers, and he and Joe had been teammates back on the A's. He got Joe over to the Brewers to help us out in spring training and to show up on the road every once in a while. So then I even got to work with Joe Rudi personally, which was a neat thing.

I grew up in Southern California. I played in a high school all-star game, Northern California against Southern California up in Candlestick Park in

San Francisco. (Hall of Famer) Eddie Murray was a teammate. That was my first chance to play in a big-league stadium. As a high school kid, that was pretty exciting. I think it was even Astroturf at the time, my first time on it, so that was a big deal.

★ ★ ★ BIG-LEAGUE MEMORIES ★ ★ ★

The World Series in 1982 was a highlight of my career. But another high-light came in the last regular-season game of the 1982 season. The Brewers were playing the Orioles in Baltimore and, ironically, after the first 161 games we were tied for first and playing each other in that last game, so basically it was a one-game playoff for the division title.

I did okay. I hit a couple of home runs off Jim Palmer, and I think I had a triple in there somewhere. It was obviously a big game for the team.

The only round of the playoffs back then was a best of five, and we had to go to Anaheim to play the Angels in the first two games and then go to Milwaukee for the last three. That's the way they did it then.

Well, we went out to Anaheim from Baltimore and we lost the first two games. So obviously going back to Milwaukee our backs were against the wall. But we were able to win three straight to get to the World Series.

And then in a very exciting World Series that went seven games, again we went to a final game, but we lost to St. Louis. We had five do-or-die games in a matter of two or three weeks and we won four of them, but the last one we couldn't pull off.

But I wouldn't trade the experience for anything. The only thing I'd change is the outcome of the seventh game. Out of the 20 years I played it was without a doubt the most exciting time for me.

Another memory I have is that I got to catch the final out of a no-hitter. Juan Nieves was pitching for us in Baltimore, and I was playing center field at the time. That was kind of fun.

Getting the 3,000th hit was pretty exciting, especially to get it in Milwaukee, where I played my whole career. It was a line-drive single to right-center off Jose Mesa.

I didn't get to play in very many All-Star games, but I had fun in the three I played in.

★★★ SUPERSTITIONS ★★★

I was like anybody else, I guess, who does this kind of stuff. If you won the day before you'd probably wear the same shoes or whatever. I was no different that way, but I wasn't a fanatic or anything out of the ordinary.

MENTAL EDGE

In many ways, the shortstop is the traffic cop on the field. Fielding grounders is only a small part of the job description.

He sees everything from his spot in the middle of the diamond. He especially takes notice of what pitch the catcher is calling. That's what starts his mind racing.

A right-handed hitter is up. He's a pull hitter, and a good fastball hitter. There's a runner on first base. The catcher calls a fastball.

Then he lets the second baseman know that he should be covering the base in case of a steal because the shortstop has to play the hitter toward the hole. He makes sure the pitcher knows who will be covering the bag for a double-play attempt on a grounder back to the mound.

The pitch is delivered, and the batter hits a high pop-up to the infield between third and short. The third baseman and the shortstop both drift toward the ball. The shortstop waves his hands and calls for the ball, taking charge as a shortstop must do when the opportunity presents itself.

He makes the catch. He gives the ball to the pitcher, delivering a brief pep talk to him as he does so. And as he returns to his position, the shortstop faces the outfielders and raises his right index finger, reminding them that there is one out.

Then he peers in to see what the catcher is calling for the next hitter, setting in motion another series of defensive directions.

A shortstop's work is never done.

—*S. K.*

GLOSSARY

Banana route: A semicircular path to field a ball, as opposed to a straight-line path.

Hole: On the left side of the infield, it's the area between where the shortstop and the third baseman play.

Range: The amount of ground a fielder can cover well going to his left and going to his right.

Squared up: Facing directly.

Target: Where you want to throw the ball.

★★★★★★★★★★★★★★★★★★★★★★★★

CONCLUSION

★★★★★★★★★★★★★★★★★★★★★★★★

You don't become a Hall of Famer by accident.

The 19 players in this book may have been born with natural baseball skills, but they each had a strong inner drive to become the best, a drive that manifested itself in good work habits as well as a studious approach to the game.

Of course, not everyone plays the same way. In becoming one of the greatest players to ever wear a big-league uniform, each Hall of Famer developed his own style and technique. And, as they suggest, every player goes through a trial and error period to learn which techniques work best.

Sure, baseball is just a game. And it's possible to just go out onto the field and let your natural skills and instincts take over.

But nothing that is worthwhile comes easily. It takes practice and hard work if you want to be the best. Baseball is no different.

Certainly not everyone who plays baseball will be a Hall of Famer. But everyone who is serious about the game can be the best player possible by following the Hall of Famers' advice.

Use your head. Be prepared. Be focused. Concentrate on what you're doing and think about how you can become even better.

That's as important as extra batting practice, or taking more ground balls, or throwing an extra bullpen session.

Think about it.

ACKNOWLEDGMENTS

This project could not have been accomplished without the cheerful, intelligent, efficient, and determined assistance and guidance from Jeff Idelson, the Hall of Fame's vice-president of communications and education.

Brad Horn, the Hall's director of public relations, was also extremely helpful in setting up interviews for the project.

There are several other people at the Hall of Fame to whom I am grateful for helping to bring this project to life, notably Dale Petroskey, president; Bill Haase, vice-president; Scot Mondore, business manager; Ted Spencer, vice-president and chief curator; and Jim Gates, librarian.

And, of course, I would like to thank the Hall of Famers themselves who accepted the invitations to become part of this project. Their insights and willingness to extend a portion of their valuable time was greatly appreciated.

Also helpful with this project were Dick Bresciani of the Boston Red Sox, and Larry Yount, as well as my Hall of Fame children, Amy, Jeff, and Emily.

STEVEN KRASNER was a sports writer for the *Providence Journal* for thirty-three years, covering the Boston Red Sox on a daily basis from 1986 until his retirement in 2008. He is a graduate of Columbia University, where he played baseball and was team captain and MVP in his senior year. Krasner is the author of PLAY BALL LIKE THE PROS: TIPS FOR KIDS FROM 20 BIG LEAGUE STARS; PLAY BALL LIKE THE HALL OF FAMERS: THE INSIDE SCOOP FROM 19 BASEBALL GREATS; PEDRO MARTINEZ; WHY NOT CALL IT COW JUICE?; THE LONGEST GAME; and HAVE A NICE NAP, HUMPHREY. He conducts interactive and motivational writing workshops called "Nudging the Imagination" (www.nudgingtheimagination.com) in schools and at conferences across the country and is a member of the Baseball Hall of Fame's Education Advisory Council. He lives in Rhode Island.